Growing Your Choral Program

Growing Your Choral Program

A Practical Guide for New Directors

Nicolás Alberto Dosman

ROWMAN & LITTLEFIELD
Lanham • Boulder • New York • London

Published by Rowman & Littlefield
An imprint of The Rowman & Littlefield Publishing Group, Inc.
4501 Forbes Blvd., Ste. 200
Lanham, MD 20706
www.rowman.com

86-90 Paul Street, London EC2A 4NE

Copyright © 2024 by The Rowman & Littlefield Publishing Group, Inc.

All rights reserved. No part of this book may be reproduced in any form or by any electronic or mechanical means, including information storage and retrieval systems, without written permission from the publisher, except by a reviewer who may quote passages in a review.

British Library Cataloguing in Publication Information Available

Library of Congress Cataloging-in-Publication Data

Names: Dosman, Nicolás Alberto, 1979- author.
Title: Growing your choral program : a practical guide for new directors / Nicolás Alberto Dosman.
Description: Lanham : Rowman & Littlefield Publishers, 2024. | Includes bibliographical references and index.
Identifiers: LCCN 2024003553 (print) | LCCN 2024003554 (ebook) | ISBN 9781538158951 (cloth) | ISBN 9781538158968 (paperback) | ISBN 9781538158975 (ebook)
Subjects: LCSH: Choirs (Music)—Management. | Choral conducting.
Classification: LCC MT88 .D68 2024 (print) | LCC MT88 (ebook) | DDC 782.5/14—dc23
LC record available at https://lccn.loc.gov/2024003553
LC ebook record available at https://lccn.loc.gov/2024003554

Contents

Preface and Acknowledgments *vii*

1 Fit: The Human Connection *1*
2 Connecting with Everyone: Are All Really Welcome? *13*
3 Ensembles: School Choruses, Church Choruses, and Community Choruses *27*
4 Skill Development and Rehearsal Priorities *39*
5 Musicianship: Developing Notational Literacy *69*
6 Program Development: Evolution of the Developing Program *79*
7 Public Relations: Community versus School Chorus *99*
8 Programming Literature: Making Your Choirs Successful *109*

Appendices *121*

Selected Bibliography *143*

Index *145*

About the Author *149*

Preface and Acknowledgments

I have had the privilege of directing choirs since 1995 at the age of fifteen when I was still in my first year of singing in high school choir. Since my time working with choirs, I have also had the opportunity to work with many wonderful choral directors from high school through my professional career as a conductor. As a chorister, I learned from the conductors; as a student and professional, I learned from my students, colleagues, teachers, and mentors.

The idea for this book was birthed not only from my experience and struggles early in my teaching career. I have had also had the privilege of working with preservice teachers and teachers entering the profession as an inspiration for this book. My former students, as well as many new teachers, need quick practical resources while they become acclimated to the profession. By no means is this text meant to be comprehensive or an authority on choral music or pedagogy. My hope is that this book will help those who, like me, struggled early in their career and needed quick practical guidance.

I am grateful for the many people who have supported me throughout my career and for the privilege of working with Drs. Judy Bower, Kevin Fenton, and André Thomas at Florida State University while I was pursuing my master's degree. The support and encouragement of Dr. Harold Abeles, professor emeritus at Teachers College, Columbia, who believed in my potential as a scholar, ensured that I had opportunities to develop as both a musician and as a researcher. I would also like to thank Michele Kaschub, professor at the University of Southern Maine, for encouraging me to pursue this project. Finally, I would like to thank my family who have always had high expectations and believed in me.

If you are new to the profession and want to serve others, I hope this book will give the guidance you need. It has been one of the greatest personal joys of my life to be a teacher and choral director. I never would have imagined that I would be "living the dream."

One

Fit
The Human Connection

"Music is my tool . . . people are my purpose."

—*André Thomas*[1]

The majority of us are in this profession because music somehow moved us in a way that transcended superficial entertainment. Each of us (hopefully) has a deep connection to music that sometimes may be difficult to express in words. For many of us, our first aesthetic experience may have been when we were in the audience. The experience of connecting with the music as an audience member may have sparked our interest in music. Therefore, if we as conductors do not take this into consideration, we are not making the effort to fully connect with others.

To be successful in this profession, we must ask ourselves: Why am I doing this? Is this the right path for me? Am I in the right place? All of us in the field have asked ourselves these questions at some point in our careers. The answers may not always be clear or may change, but the questions must be asked, nonetheless. We have the opportunity to share music with others if we are prepared to do so. Music has the potential to affect—even change—the lives of those we share it with, so we must be well-equipped to do so. We must begin this task by deep introspection and thoughtfulness.

Acquiring the necessary skills to be a competent professional musician is, of course, a prerequisite to becoming a conductor. Having strong musical instincts can only enhance what we may have learned through formal study. However, making the human connection is what will allow us to reach our ensembles and communities. The ability to connect with others, particularly in the role of a choral conductor, determines our effectiveness with the ensembles we conduct. Many of us have worked with very charismatic individuals who may not have been the most skilled conductor or had scholarly backgrounds. Despite the limitations of these conductors, the ensemble loved, and even worshipped, them, even though the ensemble's sound may have been lackluster. Many of us can also recall instances when we have sung with very qualified conductors who lacked the ability to connect with the ensemble. Imagine if their ability to connect with others matched their skill level, and then imagine the kind of experience the ensemble would have.

If we are going to make the choice to enter this profession, making the human connection is just as important as musical competency. Choral conductors need to remember singing is the most personal form of music making. While instrumentalists must deal with the physical vagaries of their instruments, singers must manage not only the physical but the intellectual, emotional, spiritual, and cultural factors affecting their instrument—the body housing their voice. Conducting individuals who share something as intimate as their voice requires an ability to connect with them to the point of inspiring them to strive for and achieve excellence.

You don't have to be an extrovert or a rockstar to do this. Robert Shaw describes his philosophy in the following manner: "I think my principle tools now are leading rather than chastising, inspiring rather than dispiriting. I am also grateful for the fact that I don't have to feel that I am false or phony about it. The music IS worth more than I am. I don't use inspiration as a tool. I think I am inspired, too. I hope it's the music speaking through me."[2]

To make the human connection, you need to allow yourself to be vulnerable. Vulnerability requires sharing not only your knowledge but yourself with the ensembles you conduct. Sharing does not mean divulging intimate details of your personal life, nor does it mean treating rehearsals as group therapy sessions. Sharing means allowing the ensemble to have a sense of your essence, your core.

Making a connection means showing an interest in the ensemble members beyond their singing. This is not a matter of solving personal problems but rather accepting the members for who they are, recognizing they each have challenges and triumphs. Empathizing with individuals during their struggles as well as celebrating their successes is how we can connect with the people in our ensembles.

Most choral ensembles consist of people who have chosen to volunteer their time for the common cause of making music. Most of us do not begin our careers conducting choral ensembles of paid professionals. Therefore, we must make sure that every rehearsal is worth their time and effort. If we do not, why should we expect them to volunteer their time and talent. One can argue that in a school setting, incentive is tied to academic progress in the class. This may be true, but even if students did not make the choice to be there, we must make the effort to connect with these individuals—especially these individuals. How we make the connection is dictated by our personality or disposition. Regardless of your temperament, it is imperative to find the unique inner qualities that will enable an ensemble to trust you to the point that they can freely share their voices in a rehearsal. This means that we must be willing to be both generous and vulnerable.

Our ensembles expect us to come prepared and to be the expert in the room, as we should be. However, being the expert does not imply infallibility or god-like qualities. True leaders own their imperfections and strive to improve. Ensembles tend to admire conductors who acknowledge their own imperfections. Moreover, this sets an example for the ensemble members to be vulnerable and open themselves to growth. Genuine vulnerability does not stem from unpreparedness, incompetence, or weakness but from the strength to acknowledge our shortcomings despite our talents or best efforts. We must be open to learning and growth: as a leader who makes the effort to be as prepared as possible. If we are not prepared to lead yet assume the role of leader, the best we can share with an ensemble is mediocrity. Vulnerability resulting from lack of preparedness comes from a place of selfishness rather than a giving place.

Only when we adopt a servant-leader approach to choral conducting can we acknowledge that the music we are preparing is not about us. We are certainly a part of the music making, but our greatest responsibility is to serve the music by making every effort to discover the composer's intent and then honoring these intentions through the ensembles we conduct. In order to accomplish this task, the conductor must know the capabilities of the ensemble and choose repertoire the singers can perform successfully.

Remember, our role as conductors is to be a conduit between the composer and the ensemble. Understanding, selecting, and creating a nurturing space for our ensemble and the repertoire that we choose for them is our primary task. If we are unable to do these things competently, our ability to succeed in making a meaningful connection related to the music will be diminished and, in some cases, nearly impossible. Some conductors may connect with their ensembles without actualizing this process through the music because they may lack the ability or desire to serve both the music and the ensemble. Relying on charisma is not enough to build a choral program. Conversely, having scholarly knowledge of choral repertoire and choral/vocal pedagogy prowess without the skill to convey this knowledge to others will not maintain the volunteers in your program for very long. Our goal as conductors should be to build upon our strengths and strive to overcome our weaknesses so that we may become the best conductors for our ensembles.

Becoming a choral conductor and making the choice to continue in this career path requires both introspection and a willingness to spend many hours working beyond the time on the podium to create musical experiences that will enrich the lives of the singers as well as our audience members. Connecting with our community members, whether that be in a school, church, or community choir setting, is as critical as connecting with the ensembles we conduct. Inspiring others goes beyond entertainment. We must program in a way that can evoke powerful aesthetic experiences for our audiences. Everyone enjoys being entertained, but we never forget aesthetically moving experiences.

What we choose for repertoire and why we make those choices should be influenced by the communities that we serve. In some instances, our decisions may be influenced by others, such as a board, committee, special event, or school administration. However, we must do our due diligence in learning about and understanding our communities on our own. Moreover, planning a program that will enrich the lives of our ensemble members and audience members alike has the capacity to generate more confidence in our ensemble members. When their friends and family members genuinely enjoy attending their concerts it can only reinforce their connection to the ensemble.

Am I Cut Out for This?

"As an educator, it is an exception to meet a young musician, singer, or composer who wants to work hard, invest time, face challenges and overcome failure to become a better musician, performer, conductor or composer."

—*Rosephanye Powell*[3]

Many of us enter choral directing by majoring in music education. Although colleges and universities are charged with the task of ensuring its music education graduates meet state and university requirements, each student must spend time reflecting on why they have chosen this path. Most individuals (and their parents) are aware that pursuing a music degree is not going to make them wealthy upon graduation. Some young people are even discouraged from pursuing music or music education degrees in favor of a more lucrative path. Many institutions do not even offer conducting degrees at the undergraduate level. Despite the perceived limitations of pursuing a career in music, specifically choral conducting, some individuals choose to forge ahead anyway. Why?

The majority of us who chose to pursue choral conducting became interested in it through singing in an ensemble. Some of us may have had the experience of working with a charismatic conductor whose superior musicianship inspired us to go down that path ourselves. Others may have discovered that they have a "natural gift" for easily identifying and addressing ensemble problems. Some may be curious about choral conducting but unsure of it as a career. If deep reflection does not yield a crystal-clear answer, this should not be discouraging. We may be left with a feeling that we are on the correct path but not fully able to express why. We should not expect to have all the answers, especially at the beginning of our careers, but we should be intellectually and emotionally curious enough to seriously reflect upon our choices.

Given the structures and traditions of most university settings, the most logical path to choral conducting, in my opinion, is through a degree in music education. This path may be less than ideal for some individuals, but it is often the only way to acquire the necessary tools (save a bachelor of music in conducting) for pursuing a career in choral conducting. However, if you have no interest in becoming an educator or working with children, this degree may not be your best path. Alternatively, you could pursue a degree in sacred music. Depending on the program, graduates can be reasonably prepared to conduct a religious ensemble, although this option is not the best choice unless you are interested in sacred music.

Finally, you can pursue a performance degree. Although this path will ensure the necessary training in performance, specific choral training, other than singing in an ensemble, is not part of the curriculum. Vocal performance curricula are designed to train solo singers and do not provide many opportunities to conduct ensembles. Furthermore, some vocal performance programs do not value choral singing and even have antagonistic relationships with the choral program. Yet, despite these limitations, some individuals have become successful choral conductors and have been able to effectively communicate their skills and training to a choral ensemble.

Auditioning for and pursuing an undergraduate degree in music is only the first step. During your studies you will be faced with the academic rigor of earning a degree in music. Some individuals will meet these challenges because their prior training and academic skills have prepared them for the degree program. Others will rise to the challenge due to grit and passion. Others will discover that they are not on the right path and will choose a different career despite their apparent innate ability. The decision to pursue a career in choral conducting is one that should evoke serious reflection during the undergraduate years and beyond. Taking classes, passing juries, and earning a degree provide the basic training for entering the profession. However, a degree in music is just the first step in your professional journey. Finding a place that fits your disposition and skill set is yet another journey.

Often, individuals leave the profession because they find themselves in a position for which they are not well-suited. Yet they may not recognize that if they were in a more suitable position, they (and their ensembles) could thrive. In the twenty-first century, very few individuals begin and end their careers in the same position. Those just entering the profession must realize this factor and be patient with themselves and the ensembles that they lead.

Being in the right place at the right time can make a difference in our professional and personal endeavors. Novices in all professions, including choral conducting, will have their growing pains. Moreover, these growing pains can make for stronger and ultimately better conductors. However, it may not always be easy to discern whether you have not been given an opportunity to grow or if you are simply in the wrong place. A newly minted choral conductor may be overwhelmed by having to take over a well-established choral program following the departure of a beloved predecessor. Rebuilding a program that is in decline or creating a new program is equally daunting. If the fit for the first position is not quite right, the learning curve will likely be steep, and the resulting discouragement may throw this career choice into question. While the immediate need for gainful employment should not be minimized, it is equally important to make career choices (if you have the luxury to do so) that are best suited to your temperament, skill set, and career goals.

The importance of having a mentor at the beginning of your career cannot be overstated (another case of the human connection coming into play). Good mentors are like mirrors. They may offer valuable advice but most of the time they should invite us to reflect upon our choices. Those initially entering the profession should find a mentor who will give practical feedback during the school-to-career transition period. Certainly, a conductor's enthusiasm, patience, and determination are key when leading an unfamiliar ensemble, but the support and perspective provided by a mentor are invaluable. Even the most seasoned conductors must make allowances for a transition period when leading a new ensemble and will often contact trusted colleagues and mentors for advice.

Connecting with a new ensemble will no doubt have its challenges. The first job may be the right place to start a career but later turn out to be the wrong place due to changing circumstances. Often novice conductors, either unsure of whether the first job they took is the right place or whether they definitely knew it was the wrong place, will accept the position anyway for economic reasons. If you find yourself in this position, you must remember you made this choice and must accept responsibility for this ensemble. Choral conductors are expected to be leaders. Less than ideal circumstances will put your leadership ability to the test, but for the ensemble's sake, you must make every effort to rise to the challenge and give the ensemble the best version of yourself. If you have limited chemistry with the ensemble, be gracious, formal, and have an appropriate sense of humor. Sarcasm, insults, yelling, and belittling jokes will not win over anybody. Ensembles resent this type of behavior and are likely to hold a grudge, especially if the conductor has not established a solid relationship with them. If ensemble members have a deeper connection with the conductor, they may be more tolerant of unintended gaffes. However, we should always be mindful of our demeanor and professional image and avoid squandering the ensemble's patience. Unless an ensemble respects the conductor as a consummate professional, deeper connections will not occur. A conductor earns respect by always being prepared and professional. Even when you have gained ground with the ensemble and are able to form deeper connections, the ensemble needs continued evidence that you are qualified and have the ability to lead.

After the first year in a new position, a period of reflection should take place, with important questions asked. What were my successes? Where could I have improved? Did I put forth my best effort? Once these questions are given serious thought and reflection, then you can ask: "Am I in the right place?" The answer may be simply "I don't know yet." If this is the case, it may be worth spending another year with the ensemble. It is likely you have developed some connections with the ensemble and have made some adjustments. If you persevere despite the challenges of year one, you can begin to implement your vision in earnest.

Making the commitment to continue in a position beyond the first year often leads to a more successful second year, when a better assessment can be made about the suitability of the position. By the second year, some of the connection issues should resolve themselves as those singers who were not going to accept new leadership will have left the ensemble, and those who remain have developed some degree of acceptance or even loyalty to you or the ensemble. The second year also opens the opportunity to avoid mistakes made in the first year and to gain a better understanding of the work environment. Although insights may have been gained in the first year, year two does not erase every issue that may be a part of the ensemble's or institution's culture. Understanding the culture of the environment can be a challenge even if the fit is a good one.

Year two may be more successful than year one, but that does not necessarily clarify things for us. We may very well be at the perfect institution for our career (at that moment in time) or not. The overarching questions that should inform our decisions at this stage are twofold: Will I continue to grow here? Will I be able to help the ensemble grow? If the answer is a convincing "No," then it is certainly time to move on, especially if circumstances are unlikely to improve. However, we must be sure that is a true "No" rather than the result of a year or two of growing pains. This distinction may be difficult to determine early in your career. This is another instance when consulting a trusted mentor can be helpful in reflecting upon your choices and in making an informed assessment of your career trajectory.

If it is time to make a career move, you should be relatively certain that the move is forward. Moving forward means finding a position that will encourage personal growth and fulfillment. What constitutes a forward move will be different for everyone and does not necessarily mean leading a more established ensemble. To some individuals, the challenge of developing a new program or rebuilding a program may be a forward move. Others will view a forward move in economic terms or in terms of better facilities, administration, and other work conditions.

Regardless of the motivations for moving on, the decision to do so should be made with a great deal of reflection and discernment. A conductor's level of professionalism can be put to the test when separating from an ensemble. Leaving gracefully and in a dignified manner should be a very high priority. Every ensemble deserves to have a smooth transition. Generally speaking, the outgoing director will not be involved in the search for a successor but can be a valuable resource to the search committee. An outgoing director should maintain distance from the search and offer appropriate advice only when it is sought. A true professional will seek to make the process as easy as possible for the ensemble, search committee, and potential successor. An outgoing conductor should speak only positively or in a neutral manner to ensemble members about the successor. Whatever disagreements you might have about the direction the ensemble is taking after your departure, speaking ill of your successor will tarnish your reputation as a professional. Remember, the position was no longer a fit; that is why you moved on. The ensemble is no longer your concern despite the connections made with its members.

Finding the right place in the twenty-first century seems to be a flexible concept. The right place could be a temporary or more long-term notion depending on the circumstances and the individuals. One of the clearest markers of being in the right place is the ability to make connections with many individuals and to have a shared vision with them. If you have good chemistry with the ensemble, board, or administrators, and everyone embraces the same vision, then it is likely that you are in the right place. Under these circumstances, it is possible to experience personal growth and facilitate growth in an ensemble. As long as this continues to be the case, you should seriously consider building a career at that organization or institution. Barring personal circumstances (yes, life happens!), it is to your benefit to stay in such a position unless the circumstances change, or you are not adequately compensated.

When you land the perfect choral conducting job, initial feelings of elation and excitement can make the first year thrilling rather than daunting. However, even the ideal position requires hard work and will present its challenges. Having an ensemble that trusts your instincts and an administration or board that follows suit makes meeting those challenges easier. Despite these positive circumstances, financial limitations, personality conflicts, and the ensemble's limitations will still be factors in any position. Navigating these factors is simply a part of life and will be encountered in any work environment. Professionalism and flexibility will still determine how long a position remains the right place. Flexibility and compromise will always be necessary, no matter how seemingly perfect a job might be, but compromising your vision or standards of excellence should not be considered.

Vision and standards are defining characteristics of a conductor's identity. It is the conductor's responsibility to ignite and excite the ensemble members about their own vision and to help them rise to the standards necessary to realize that vision. Usually, resistance to a vision comes from an administration or board that, in all likelihood, is made up of non-musicians. A conductor can either weather the storm or move on. Leaving under these circumstances tends to be more difficult and painful for both the ensemble and conductor because of the personal and musical bonds that have been cultivated. Bearing up under a conflictive, or even an abusive, administration has the potential to drive one out of the profession entirely, and it may be best to make music elsewhere. Enduring abuse is not grit; it is allowing oneself to be victimized.

Entering the profession of choral conducting has been one of the greatest privileges of my life. The ensembles I have worked with share extraordinary personal gifts: their voices. They have placed their trust in me, and this is very humbling, regardless of the skill level or age of the singers. Because of this tremendous responsibility, upon embarking on my career, I found myself asking: Am I cut out for this? Am I in the right place? For years, I have asked these questions and have continued to reflect upon my career choices and trajectory. Impostor syndrome, or feeling of self-doubt, has crept into and sometimes still creeps into my psyche. The most effective conductors I have observed still love what they do, and their love for music and music making is infectious.

At the start of my career, I was exhilarated but encountered many challenges that brought about self-doubt. Despite the initial self-doubt, I knew I was following a calling from deep within. I am more excited about my career choice now and, of course, more experienced. One of the most fulfilling aspects of my career has been, and continues to be, connecting with others through music. When we find a position that is a personal fit as well as a fit for the ensemble, connecting with the ensemble members becomes much easier. We choral conductors are charged to teach our ensembles, but, in that process, we learn a great deal from them, shaping who we are and who we become.

As we grow into our identity, we must make sure that our growth allows others to grow and be themselves as well. A true leader is secure enough within their core and is open enough to development so that they can create a space for others to grow as well. The choral ensemble and atmosphere should suit not only us but also the individuals who are a part of the whole. All of our chorus members should feel that they belong and can thrive within the ensemble. If not, individuals will leave the ensemble, or the environment may become toxic. One challenging aspect of leading a group is working with a diverse group and allowing all to feel equally valued, especially those individuals we disagree with or don't understand. However, if we can respect each other we will grow, and our ensembles will be enriched by such diversity. The best career matches for choral directors and educators are ones where the director and the ensemble can grow together.

Notes

1. Brown, Marina, 2017, "Andre Thomas: 'Music Is My Tool . . . People Are My Purpose.'" *Tallahassee Democrat*, April 28, https://www.tallahassee.com/story/life/2017/04/28/andre-thomas-music-my-tool-people-my-purpose/100853982/.

2. Robert Shaw, "Quotes from Contributors," https://robertshaw.website/shaw-quotes.

3. Rosephanye Powell, "Homepage," https://www.rosephanyepowell.com/.

Two

Connecting with Everyone
Are All Really Welcome?

Chapter 2 addresses how we as choral directors create an environment that welcomes a diverse population. Although this chapter is not intended to be a silver bullet or meant to solve every issue, it will address ways to create a welcoming environment for LGBTQ and BIPOC individuals as well to address our responsibility to use music to promote social justice.

"Injustice anywhere is a threat to justice everywhere. We are caught in an inescapable network of mutuality, tied in a single garment of destiny. Whatever affects one directly, affects all indirectly."

—*Martin Luther King Jr.*

Many of us, leaders and singers, join an ensemble because we want to be a part of a community. Our profession promotes the idea that choral ensembles should be places where all are welcome. In recent years, the American Choral Directors Association at regional and national levels has offered many diversity, equity, and inclusion initiatives as a part of its mission, and sometimes conferences present themes around inclusivity. In fact, the American Choral Directors Association 2023 conference theme was "A Place of Belonging." The 2023 conference included immersion choirs focused on the music of Latin America, the Black diaspora, Indigenous people, and jazz. Sessions also included workshops that specifically addressed the LGBTQIA+ community. These initiatives are commendable and show progress within the field. Later that year, the National Collegiate

Choral Organization held its conference in Atlanta, Georgia, at Morehouse College, a historically Black college. The conference featured choirs from Historically Black Colleges and Universities as well as sessions focused on diversity and the history and legacy of Historically Black College and University choirs.

However, we still must grapple with a very important question within our profession: Are all really welcome? Does everyone have a place at the table? On the surface this question may seem rhetorical, but if we examine our practice as choral conductors/educators and the profession as a whole, have we really embraced diversity? How much progress have we made as a profession? It is my belief that our programming is a reflection of our values, at least musically. How many choral concerts consist of repertoire composed by males of European descent that walked the earth hundreds of years ago? How many choral concerts present a majority of female composers or other underrepresented composers? How many concerts include religiously diverse music beyond Christianity, besides the token "Channukah song" or Hebrew song during the holidays that may or may not even be related to Channukah? We champion diversity at conferences or in theory, but do the majority of choral programs in the United States consistently program music that is diverse in a balanced way? Those who are open to change may want to reflect upon our individual programming and what is programmed by the profession as a whole. Where are we on this journey? Have we even begun the journey? Do we really care? Should we care? Concert programming is only one aspect of creating a welcoming environment. However, what we program will give the public a sense of how inclusive we are to diverse voices.

The concept of diversity has evolved over time. *Oxford Dictionary* defines the word diversity as follows: "the quality or fact of including a range of many people or things." Was the concept of diversity in 1924 the same as it is in 2024, 1964 versus 2024, or even 2014 versus 2024? Most of us would agree that the notion of diversity has broadened over time. The United States has become a more diverse country over time. According to the US Census[1] in 1923, the first instance of forced diversification was when European invaders had arrived in the Americas, before the United

States was even formed, then originally inhabited by the Indigenous nations. Subsequently, the Europeans conquered this territory and formed new nations with new identities and all but eliminated or marginalized the original inhabitants and their descendants. The United States of America in its origins was a nation that was predominantly of European descendants after the subjugation of the Indigenous people. In fact, males of European descent were the only individuals who were considered full citizens of the United States for a considerable period of time. Despite this reality, even in this country's infancy, racial and ethnic diversity had always existed even if racial and ethnic minorities did not have a voice for much of this country's history.

In 2008, the United States of America elected its first Black president and in 2020 elected its first female vice president of Black and Asian descent. Despite individuals with diverse backgrounds holding the very highest offices, including the head of state, diversity and inclusion are still challenging topics. Many still struggle with understanding how non-white individuals can rise to the highest levels of government while discrimination still exists. It may seem paradoxical to many. Even though slavery still seems something out of the past, Daniel Smith, who is believed to be the last child of a former slave, died at age ninety in 2022. This very fact demonstrates that slavery based on race in the United States may be part of the past, but it is a past that is not so distant. Racial and ethnic diversity has always existed in the United States, but the concepts of equality and inclusion are fairly new concepts to this nation despite its apparent progress.

One could make the case that much of the popular and commercial music of the twentieth and twenty-first century would not exist if it weren't for African American music and culture. Despite the sordid history of the United States, music inevitably found its way to be inclusive. Although society made its best efforts to segregate and dehumanize people, music found a way to integrate and to some extent humanize cultures that would otherwise be segregated. However, "mainstream" choral music for the greater part of the twentieth century and part of the twenty-first century highlighted music composed and conducted by European men. Discussions about multiculturalism have been an ongoing interest in music education organizations such as the National Association for Music Education (formerly the Music Educators National Conference), which can be found in the Housewright Symposium and Vision 2020 documents; these documents and discussions leading to the creation of these documents, albeit very significant and a step forward, did not lead to the profession instantly changing its practices or philosophy.

Understanding exactly where we are as a nation and profession, and where communities are, is the first step in our attempt to approach diverse programming in an authentic way. Diverse programming that is truly inclusive is an ongoing process. Some choral directors are genuinely interested in programming music but are concerned that they may appropriate the music of cultural groups they do not belong to. Others simply do not prioritize it or consider non-Western music or music by people of color "special music" and will include it as a "fun" piece. In some cases, others inadvertently caricaturize or appropriate music that is considered to be "ethnic." The American Choral Directors Association has a standing committee focused on diversity initiatives. This standing committee is one of many resources that choral directors can take advantage of. With the advances of modern technology and the internet, most choral directors have the ability to research the music and performance practice of other cultures. The only reason diversity is not a part of every choral program in an authentic way is due to a lack of interest. If we conduct an ensemble with diverse individuals, it may be challenging to program culturally diverse music especially if we do not belong to a diverse group, but that should not be a barrier. That can be seen as an opportunity for connection and mutual learning. We can call upon, when appropriate, experts within the community to help guide us.

Conducting an ethnically diverse ensemble may bring the need to program music outside the "Western canon" to the forefront. Conversely, more homogenous ensembles should have culturally diverse music included as well; it will also enrich their ensembles and musical vocabulary. When we make the choice to program music outside of our culture we may want to consult with experts. The experts may be members of our own ensemble, a member of our community, or an outside source. It may be worth noting that belonging to a given cultural group does not necessarily make one a musical expert. If we do not assume that individuals of European descent are born scholars of Western European music, we should not assume that ethnic minorities are experts in music of their cultural heritage. However, within the culture of the United States, a rich tradition of choral singing exists in the African American community. This tradition has evolved over time, and there are scholars and available scholarly resources that focus specifically on African American musical traditions. Marques Garrett's *The Oxford Book of Choral Music by Black Composers* is one resource every choral conductor should have.

Due to the complicated history of the United States and the perseverance of African Americans, the African American Church, and Historically Black Colleges and Universities, the African American choral tradition was able to survive and thrive alongside the European/European American choral tradition. Choral directors wishing to program African American music have a multitude of authentic resources to successfully do so. Despite being an individual who identifies as Black (Afro-Latino), I had to research and continue to study African American music and learn about the style and performance practice of different genres. Despite my cultural heritage, many assume that I am an expert in the African American musical traditions simply because of my skin color. I have programmed African American music with choirs that had no African American individuals in the choir and did so confidently. I will continue to program this music because African American music is American music and has artistic value. I have attended conferences where non-Black individuals have had reservations about programming music of this tradition and at times appeared to seek permission to do so. In one instance, André Thomas, author of *Way Over Beulah Land*, informed the predominantly white attendees that approaching the African American choral tradition with the same level of respect and scholarship that one would study other genres was very important. Moreover, he assured this group that anyone can perform and conduct African American music authentically if they are well informed and prepared to do so.

Choral directors should not be afraid to program or conduct genres or music of other cultures simply because they do not belong to the group. Technology allows us to connect with cultural experts in most areas of the world. We can bring these experts and composers into our rehearsals to give us and our ensembles feedback. I have done so and many of my colleagues do so. Additionally, university scholars can help inform our approach in the same way we might consult a musicologist for appropriate performance practice of Western ensembles or an ethnomusicologist for world music genres. Including music of other cultures, races, ethnicities, or nationalities is already a part of our practice even if we may not be aware of it. How many of us program music by German, English, Italian, and French composers but do not identify with these nationalities? The difference between programming composers of these nationalities as opposed to other composers lies in our preparation and knowledge of this genre. Schools of music and conservatories have trained a majority of students to perform music by European male composers by virtue of the curricula design at these institutions. Broadening our horizons and doing the requisite study and research allows us to program more diverse music without fear of appropriation. We can use our training to learn about other styles and performance practice. When committed to doing this, we can create a much more inclusive environment for our ensemble members as well as introduce them to music they may have never even imagined performing. When we program music for our ensembles, we should always consider the individuals that participate in our ensembles first. Programming diverse repertoire is only the first step. We must make the effort to understand the story, journey, and struggles of our ensemble members, particularly if we come from a place of privilege and our ensemble members belong to a marginalized group. Racial and ethnic diversity is only one facet of the diversity we may encounter within our ensembles. We also have diversity of gender and sexuality that must be considered and that may require more nuance. Programming music by female composers, albeit important, does not fully include diversity in terms of gender and sexuality.

Some in our profession may think that gender and sexuality issues may be irrelevant to choral ensembles and directors should not trouble themselves with this subject because it is a personal or private matter. In some parts of the United States, many believe that individuals who identify as transgender do not sing in their ensembles. Others believe that acknowledging their existence will alienate other members and create an issue that in their eyes never really existed. However, being unaware of individuals who identify as transgender does not mean that they do not exist in our ensembles, or if they do, they are not a part of the ensemble. Approximately 5 percent of young adults identify as transgender in the United States according to the Pew Research Center.[2] Whether or not we are aware of their presence in our ensembles, individuals who identify as transgender contribute to our ensembles. According to Joshua Palkki, "Choral teachers and other education professionals who wish to be openly affirming of trans students may need to carefully consider their specific contexts, including the state and community in which they live."[3] The communities that we work in may or may not support efforts to be inclusive. Given the polarization of the United States, this reality should not come as a surprise. Despite this polarization, our ensembles may be the only place some individuals feel that they belong. It is our responsibility to provide inclusive places, especially in school or youth choirs.

Regardless of our stance on LGBTQIA+ issues, many in our profession of education would agree that when a young person takes their own life it is especially tragic. According to the Trevor Project, 45 percent of LGBTQ youth seriously considered suicide in 2022 and nearly one in five transgender and nonbinary youth attempted suicide. Moreover, more than 60 percent of LGBTQ youth said their home was not affirming.[4] These numbers should alarm anyone, regardless of one's viewpoint or background. While some of us are better equipped than others to create an environment where LGBTQ individuals are included, others may find it challenging because we do not have the requisite knowledge to create an inclusive atmosphere, particularly when it comes to individuals who identify as transgender or nonbinary. Those of us who were born in the twentieth century were likely raised in a binary, heteronormative environment. This may explain our lack of exposure or awareness. However, it does not absolve us of providing an ensemble where all of our choristers can feel safe and belong.

Many of us who are more open minded, or even those who belong to the LGBTQ community, may find it difficult to be inclusive because we are not prepared to do so on a social or instructional level. If the culture of our ensembles is gendered in terms of attire and ensembles (men's chorus/women's chorus) and we refer to our tenors and basses as men and our sopranos and altos as women, we may want to reconsider these practices. Moreover, we may have limitations in our ability to pedagogically address our transgender or nonbinary individuals in the ensemble, particularly when addressing the voice and their vocal needs. In some current practices, we may be unable to fully address without causing significant disruption to our ensembles. However, we can adapt certain behaviors immediately. One easy way involves how we refer to our tenors/basses and sopranos/altos: Do we really need to call them men/women? Can we call them by section or lower voices versus treble voices? If this seems too difficult because we associate sopranos and altos as females—is this true in a boy's choir with sopranos and altos? Conversely, how many of us conduct cisgender females who sing tenor in our choirs on occasion? It may seem difficult at first to change but not all change is as difficult as our perception allows. In my experience, I have found that any step, however small, to acknowledge and include gender diversity is welcome by the choirs I have worked with. At the same time, we must acknowledge that some of our efforts, however well meaning, will not be enough, and we may fall short. Despite our limitations and shortcomings, we should not give up on evolving—when we know better, we can and should do better. An important lesson I have learned is to avoid making assumptions, especially about the feelings of others.

Palkki also states that: "Some trans singers may revel in the fact that their voice does not match society's notions of how their voice should sound. Other trans people consider the voice a vital way that they 'do' their gender in society. Choral music educators can determine through conversation the level of connection, if any, between a trans student's voice and gender identity."[5] This statement requires us to vanquish any preconceived notions and forces us to recognize that transgender/nonbinary individuals are not a monolith. The nature of an ensemble director is to think about the group and to categorize individuals. However, we must recognize that no two individuals are the same and that each individual is on a unique and very personal journey especially when it comes to the voice. I have found that this is not only the best approach but the only approach to have with my ensemble members. None of my academic or musical training or preparation had prepared me for addressing the needs of transgender individuals, but that is a shortcoming of my education and preparation. My singers should not have to suffer due to my lack of preparation or wisdom. As a profession, we have only begun to consider the needs of our non-gender-conforming students. Many of us, including those with the best intentions, have sometimes oversimplified the connection between voice and identity. Each individual's voice is unique and a singer's connection to the voice and its implications may or may not pertain to their personal gender identity. To assume that a transgender female would automatically want to sing in falsetto until they have fully transitioned may be a false and potentially damaging assumption. Conversely, to insist that a transgender male sing as soprano because it is "their instrument" could be emotionally harmful to that individual. There is no one solution that will be appropriate for all individuals, and we must be willing to accept that as a starting point.

As I stated earlier, I did not receive the necessary preparation to address the needs of transgender and nonbinary individuals in my undergraduate education and even later in my graduate education. I suspect many of us educated in the twentieth or early twenty-first century find ourselves in the same predicament. However, it is important for us to address not only the pedagogical and physiological needs of our singers but also the psychological and socioemotional needs as well. For some non-gender-conforming students, the choral ensemble may be the only place they feel safe. Insisting they sing a voice part that is psychologically unsuitable for them can do more harm than good, despite our intentions. Moreover, if we do so without consulting them and taking their needs into account, we may alienate them and drive them out of our ensembles. Conversely, we are the vocal experts and must avoid putting singers in a situation where they are assigned to a part they physically cannot sing or might do them harm. In most cases, if we remain open minded and create a space where our singers feel safe and comfortable, we should be able to find a place for all our singers, regardless of their gender identity. Personally speaking, it was challenging for me at first, not because I did not want to be inclusive, but I simply was unaware of what to do, until I was made aware in an unexpected way.

Upon completing graduate school and embarking on a new career in rural New England, I became aware of the presence of transgender/nonbinary individuals in choral ensembles for the very first time. It was especially shocking for me when I learned that my colleagues worked with openly transgender/nonbinary individuals in choral ensembles as young as middle school. If I had this discussion with my colleagues in New York or Miami this would have been less surprising, but it would have been a surprise at that time to have a discussion about middle schoolers identifying as transgender/nonbinary. As a collegiate director I have had students in my ensembles who were openly nonbinary or transgender in each ensemble every year. I felt more prepared for students in this age range to be transgender or nonbinary. At one of the institutions where I was employed, we had to adopt changes for inclusivity and bring the choral program into the twenty-first century, including changing our attire, language, as well as reimagining who can sing what voice parts. All these adjustments were not easy but necessary to create a welcoming environment. As professionals we must evolve, making every effort to serve our ensembles to our fullest potential. We can learn from our choristers: it is not their responsibility to educate us; it is our responsibility to learn as much as we can, to give everyone in our ensemble our very best.

I have educated myself in several ways by understanding that there is always more to learn. For example, I regularly consult with the voice instructors of transitioning students to discuss the best voice part for them and have always allowed room for flexibility. One of my ensemble members in pretransition was a mezzo/contralto, who eventually became a tenor, and eventually gave their junior recital as a baritone. Although this drastic change may seem unusual, it was the natural progression for this student.

As choral conductors, we are focused on the needs of the ensemble, but the needs of the individual affect the climate of the ensemble. With the exception of choruses in the Gay and Lesbian Association of Choruses, the inclusion and consideration of the needs of LGBTQ individuals in the choral setting is fairly new. Programming music that is inclusive of their experiences needs to be a part of what we do as professionals. One well-known work that specifically addresses the experience of LGBT individuals is *Considering Matthew Shepard* composed by Craig Hella Johnson in 2016. One could make the case that the murder of Matthew Shepard in 1998 was the first time that society in the United States of America appeared to be outraged at the brutal murder of an individual because of his sexual orientation. For the first time, individuals of all political and religious points of view collectively agreed that this crime was not acceptable. LGBTQ individuals have been a part of the fabric of the world even if they have been in the shadows for most of human history. *Considering Matthew Shepard*, the first large-scale work to address one aspect of the LGBTQ experience, was composed as recently as 2016. The year of composition of a work of this scale may not be a reflection of the presence of LGBTQ individuals in society but rather a reflection of our profession becoming increasingly open to include their experience in the choral canon.

LGBTQ individuals did not suddenly appear in our choral ensembles, even though we are only beginning to address their experiences. We have a responsibility to be inclusive and respect their vocal and psychological needs. Depending on our respective communities, we will either lead on this issue or a plan may already exist. If we do not feel prepared to lead, resources now exist in our profession to help guide us. Ultimately, our choral ensembles should be a place where all can belong. If this truly is our philosophy, we will make it known to our ensemble members in word and deed.

Diversity, equity, and inclusion are terms that have evolved over the years. The inclusion and integration of racial and ethnic cultures are quite different from addressing gender diversity. Music, art, and other cultural markers have been celebrated (or appropriated in some cases) in society. Gender diversity, beyond the traditional binary model, is relatively new for most of society. As choral conductors we can be musically inclusive of other cultures and promote female, transgender, and nonbinary composers. However, we have limited musical options when it comes to being musically inclusive of gender diversity. Moreover, racial and ethnic minorities are more visible while LGBTQ individuals may have had to live in the shadows (or continue to do so) for years. Although these differences may be apparent, it is worth noting them explicitly. Some individuals in our profession, however well intentioned, may employ a one-size-fits-all approach when addressing any kind of minority group, without regard to the unique characteristics and challenges that each group faces. Some individuals may belong to a marginalized group but fail to realize they may be privileged in other ways. Being a member of a marginalized group may allow us to empathize to a certain extent, but we can never fully understand the experience of a group that we do not belong to. Having open minds, hearts, and ears is a starting point. It may be difficult to change our practices or traditions for the sake of inclusion, but it is necessary for our profession to move forward. Some in our profession believe that these issues can be addressed in a broad sweeping manner; however, things are not so simple. Working toward having an inclusive ensemble environment is a conscious effort that we must make each and every day.

Making a conscious effort to be inclusive requires us to be as up to date as we can be and aware of the communities we serve. Many professional choral organizations offer opportunities for us to learn and educate ourselves from researchers and experts who can inform us of best practices in our field. Additionally, at many institutions there are professional development opportunities available. Technology offers opportunities that would have not been possible in the past. In my experience, I have found that experts are more than happy to share their expertise, especially in educational settings. We may not get it right all of the time, but we should always strive to do our best.

Notes

1. US Census Bureau, "Statistical Abstract of the United States," https://www2.census.gov/prod2/statcomp/documents/1921-02.pdf.

2. Anna Brown, 2022, "About 5% of Young Adults in the U.S. Say Their Gender Is Different from Their Sex Assigned at Birth," June 7, Pew Research Center,

https://www.pewresearch.org/fact-tank/2022/06/07/about-5-of-young-adults-in-the-u-s-say-their-gender-is-different-from-their-sex-assigned-at-birth/.

3. J. Palkki, 2017, "Inclusivity in Action: Transgender Students in the Choral Classroom," *Choral Journal* (57) 11: 10–34.

4. The Trevor Project, 2020, "The Trevor Project—Saving Young LGBTQ Lives," https://www.thetrevorproject.org/.

5. Palkki, "Inclusivity in Action," 20–35.

Three

Ensembles
School Choruses, Church Choruses, and Community Choruses

Chapter 3 identifies the types of ensembles a choral conductor is likely to encounter, describes the characteristics of each type, and explains how a director's expectations and approaches to solving problems of vocal production differ from one type of ensemble to another.

"You sing first with your ears, then your heart, mind, and voice."

—Margaret Hillis[1]

We can conduct many types of choirs in our profession, ranging from school choirs to professional choirs. This chapter will focus on the following choirs: school choirs, church choirs, and community choirs. School choirs tend to be the most stable form of full-time employment for choir directors. Although the salaries will vary from community to community, employment within a school system brings with it benefits and structure. Employment as a church choir director in many cases is part time and generally does not offer the same fringe benefits that a school job may. However, large congregations or well-established churches often employ a full-time music director whose responsibility is to not only direct the choir(s) but oversee an entire music ministry. Community choirs are designed to serve the members of the community. They exist for the sole purpose of making choral music. Although they may not offer the same degree of stability and structure that school or church choirs offer, directors often have more freedom to be creative with their artistic vision.

School Choirs

Elementary Level

School choirs exist primarily as a vehicle for providing a musical education to students. Depending on the community, school choirs can be very structured with a well-defined curriculum and feeder pattern, or they can be loosely structured where the individual directors invent or reinvent curricula. Some school systems have a fine arts requirement at the middle and/or high school level that a choir may or may not satisfy. Others have no such requirement. In many schools, music is required at the elementary level in the form of general music. Although singing may be a part of the general music curriculum, choir is usually an outside or extracurricular activity. Moreover, general music classes may only meet once or twice a week if offered at all.

Elementary choirs generally do not meet as a class in the same way that choirs meet at the secondary level. Often, these choirs exist as a once-a-week club where students can elect to participate if they have parents who provide transportation for them. Most of the time the directors of these choirs are the music teachers at the school and choose this undertaking in exchange for a supplement or sometimes voluntarily to give children an additional musical experience. Although it may be altruistic to offer this voluntarily, school administration will often call upon this group for various functions, which means it may have value. Unless this responsibility is explicitly part of one's responsibilities, one should be compensated for directing an auxiliary choir. Offering experiences like this to students without being compensated, however noble, essentially gives administrators permission to devalue what we do as teachers and artists.

Teaching elementary-aged children to sing is perhaps one of the most valuable things one can do to promote a musically fulfilling life. Therefore, making sure the experience is a positive one for all, especially the musically insecure singer, is paramount. Having a clear philosophy about what the goals and expectations are and easily explained to parents and administrators is very important. At what age or grade level are children allowed to join choir? Will there be multiple choirs? Is this designed to be a high-level performance ensemble or meant to provide an additional musical experience for children beyond general music? Will students be auditioned? Is the audition designed to assess the skills and ability of each child or is it part of an admissions process? If the audition is designed to be an admissions audition, are you prepared to explain your process to parents and administrators? These are fundamental questions to consider before undertaking any choir, especially at the elementary level. Given the age of elementary school children, parents will likely be much more involved and active, advocating for their children more frequently and rigorously. Having a clearly defined criteria and well-articulated philosophy will reassure parents and administrators alike that all children are being treated fairly.

Leading an elementary choir requires the director to be a master of management and pacing. Children must be actively engaged at almost every moment of the rehearsal. Even the most well-behaved children may resort to off-task behavior if the director has not planned a well-paced rehearsal. The length of rehearsals should be no more than an hour. However long your rehearsals last, musicianship should be included as this assists in skill building and pacing. Including notational reading, ear training, and other musical skills will only enhance their experience. Logistically speaking, managing children at concerts may require the assistance of parents or other adults, depending on the size of the choir. Having a core group of adults to assist with performances will make the director's life much easier and will also give parents an opportunity to be more involved without a large time commitment. As children advance to middle and high school, parental help will still be needed but the needs will change.

Middle School

Parental involvement during the middle school years may diminish as children evolve into teenagers. However, parental involvement can be helpful even in middle and high school. Middle school children are experiencing academic independence for the first time in their school career but are still under the guidance and care of their parents. It is perhaps at the middle school level where choir first becomes legitimized as a class. Students may elect to join ensembles as part of the curriculum, and many will do so because they simply enjoy singing. However, some may elect to join band or orchestra instead of choir because they may want new musical experiences. Directors often must recruit students into the class or teach students who may not want to participate. Whatever the case, children at this age are selecting courses for the first time and most are expecting their electives to be enjoyable and a relief from science, technology, engineering, and mathematics courses. This does not mean that chorus or music should be any less rigorous but should challenge a different part of their intellect and awaken artistic and creative thought.

Middle school choirs can be very rewarding choirs to work with if the teacher is progress oriented rather than product oriented. Choosing appropriate repertoire and remaining flexible is a requirement for success with this age group. As students ascend through the middle school ranks, their behavior and attitude toward adults will undoubtedly change. They may begin as sixth graders inclined to please the teacher but grow into teenagers who question authority and are at the beginning of young adulthood. In my experience, the physical changes between sixth graders and eighth graders (and witnessing those changes) were quite drastic. Some students were much smaller than I was in sixth grade and by the time they were in eighth grade were bigger and stronger than me! Classroom management, teaching social skills, appropriate behavior, and pacing supersede musical goals at this age. This is the age when they truly explore their boundaries as their bodies, minds, and voices grow through very dramatic periods of their life.

Choosing repertoire that can accommodate the changing voice, particularly the voices of evolving tenors and basses, can be challenging. Recruiting and retaining middle schoolers as they become tenors and basses can also be a challenge. Gender identity and sexual orientation may add to this challenge, according to Palkki.[2] Moreover, research indicates that if a positive musical image was not fostered in the elementary years, cisgender males may not participate in singing or music in future years.[3] With so many confounding factors, middle school choir directors may face the greatest demands.

Building rapport with the students at this age is the most important part of one's job. Rapport building means that we are a safe adult for them. We have clear expectations and accept them for who they are and can appreciate this period in their lifetime. Many colleagues I have encountered who have avoided middle school teaching did so because they were unwilling to appreciate the unique nature of working with middle schoolers. Creating a wonderful musical performance should be part of our goals with any choir. However, ensuring that they have a positive experience and healthy musical self-image is more important. Middle school–aged singers are capable of outstanding music making, but that will only happen if there is a strong bond between the teacher and students.

High School Choirs

High school students are at the beginning of young adulthood. Many are capable of independent music making and have established their musical interests. If they participate in band, orchestra, or choir they would have likely participated in those ensembles in middle school. However, choir may have room for late beginners in the school curriculum. How many individuals began singing in high school choir without any prior singing experience and became respectable singers? In fact, I did not begin singing in choir until my sophomore year of high school. Although some may begin learning instruments in high school, it may be more challenging for them to adjust to playing with more sophisticated players. In fact, many instrumentalists who join choir often contribute to the ensemble because of their strong reading skills, even if they lack singing technique.

Similar to middle school teachers, high school teachers usually must recruit students and build their classes. Unfortunately, with the demands of science, technology, engineering, mathematics, and Advanced Placement courses, college requirements, and so forth, recruiting students for their entire high school career may be more challenging than it was ten or twenty years ago. High school choral directors must advocate for their programs on various levels. They must convince the guidance counselors that their class is valuable and make accommodations for scheduling and that their program is a valuable asset to the school, deserving support, while delivering a product that reinforces this premise. Finally, parents who want to ensure that their child attends the most prestigious university in the world may also need to be convinced that choir is a place that will help their child achieve this goal. These can be very challenging circumstances to face, but knowing who the key players are within the school and cultivating relationships with these individuals will go a long way.

Philosophically speaking, we should be process oriented and should focus on the continued growth of our singers musically, socially, emotionally, and intellectually. However, the students and community are expecting accessible music that is ready to perform at a moment's notice: being able to do this is crucial. High school–level arts, much like athletic teams, are a public part of the identity and image of the school. Although the parents and administrators are not musical experts, they will hear the difference between a good performance and a poor performance. Moreover, students will want to associate with a quality program, and the reputation of the program will undoubtedly affect recruitment efforts. Given these facts, it is essential that high school choral ensembles perform as well as they are capable even if it is a work in progress.

Programming music that is ready to go at the beginning of the year may be difficult but not impossible. One of my very first performances was three weeks after school had started at a high school with a fledgling choral program. Community support was nil, and student interest was very low. Given the short timeline, the insistence of the administration that we perform, and the limitations of the students at the time, I chose a small ensemble to perform a simple canon. The performance was a success despite the simplicity of the piece because they performed well. The parents, students, and administrators were satisfied with the performance at that time. In chapter 8, I have included repertoire suggestions for developing choirs that may be useful for directors who find themselves in a similar situation.

Church Choirs

Church choirs by definition have a specific ministry and function. Many church choir directors are required to hold three positions: choral director, organist, and music director. In some churches, these are separate positions. An individual may hold two out of the three positions but in smaller churches and even some larger churches, the church choir director must be able to fulfill the job requirements for all these positions. Unlike school choirs, the focus is religious, and their purpose is to enhance the worship experience. Church choirs range in age, size, and ability level. Depending on the religious affiliation, traditional choral music may be appropriate but more contemporary music may be preferred. Those who seek positions as church choir directors must accept that their job is to promote the church and faith tradition that they are working with even if they do not share the same beliefs. Fine music making, pleasant individuals, and compensation will not overcome deep-rooted fundamental conflicts with the faith tradition. For example, for some living in a same-sex marriage when the church they work for is vehemently anti-gay could be a serious conflict. Unfortunately, major conflicts with one's life and beliefs and one's place of employment usually takes a serious emotional toll on most people. However, many church musicians belong to the faith tradition that employs them. Regardless of the circumstances, it is important to respect the faith practice and demonstrate to their choir members that their music director respects their faith.

Programming music is centered on the worship scheduled for the week. It would be wise for the music director to consult with their pastor or the administration of their church to determine what their vision and preference is for the music ministry. Ideally, the music director and pastor should have a similar vision for music ministry; if this is not the case, the music director should be willing to compromise and/or present an alternative vision that the pastor will accept. The choir members must also be onboard with the musical vision of the pastor and music director for the choir to be successful. Most church choirs do not have the ability to pay choir members; however, some have paid section leaders and instrumentalists and rely on volunteers who are motivated to contribute their time and talent to music ministry. Once a clear musical vision is established, the music director can plan for a successful season. The weekly practice of the group and expected attendance will also affect the quality and quantity of how a musical vision may be realized. If a choir only meets an hour or so before the service, there is a limited time to accomplish note learning, much less address musical nuances immediately before the service. A choir with a weekly rehearsal aside from a Sunday or Saturday rehearsal before the service will be able to learn more and reinforce material prior to the weekly services.

Planning for weekly services is vastly different from planning a concert season. In traditions such as the Roman Catholic, Anglican, or Lutheran faiths, the services are structured in a Mass format or similar liturgy. Therefore, some of the music planning is repeated at each service, depending on the liturgical calendar and norms. However, other portions of the service require the choir to learn a new selection or sing music that usually is not sung the following week. In some faith traditions, preparing a special anthem that showcases the choir and highlights a biblical reading, homily, sermon, or message for the week is expected. If the church choir is experienced and has a vast repertoire, the task becomes much easier. In the case of a developing, inexperienced choir, or one reconstituting itself, the choir director must find accessible, meaningful music for the week that the members will enjoy learning.

When teaching new repertoire to a choir, particularly something more challenging in nature, it is essential that they have enough time to prepare the piece. A new piece should not be presented in the service the same week it is prepared. Ideally the director would have a month to introduce a new choral anthem. A month of preparation gives the choir an opportunity to learn pitches and rhythms, musical nuance, as well address the spiritual context of the piece. Some choirs choose to have a holiday pageant in addition to their weekly service as a fundraiser for the choir. If these outside concerts are established and the choir enjoys performing them, it would be wise for a new director to continue with those traditions. However, it may be prudent for a new director to focus on developing the choir's skills and abilities for regular services and high holy days before introducing standalone concerts, particularly if this is not part of the choir's tradition and it does not have an established choral culture. Remember: the purpose of church choirs is to worship through music and use music to enhance the worship experience for others. Concert experiences can be wonderful for church choir members but are not the primary function of a church choir.

Community Choirs

"I like the community of choir. You're joining together with one purpose—to bring some joy to the world or to share a story of a given poet and composer."

—*Rosephanye Powell*[4]

Community choirs are the perfect choirs for individuals who wish to sing in choirs outside of a worship setting. In the context of this book, community choir will be focused on groups designed for the sake of choral singing as a primary goal. Many groups such as social justice choirs, LGBTQ choral groups, and so forth, are wonderful organizations and do serve the community, but they require their members to belong to a group or embrace a mission, albeit non-religious. Community choirs in the context of this book are non-auditioned groups with no political or religious affiliation and are open to the public. Community choir members are generally adults who wish to sing in a choir and make music. Many may have sung in their high school choir and wish to continue singing. Others may be exploring singing for the first time. It can be exciting to work with a diverse group of individuals who are dedicated to making choral music. It can also be challenging. Whether the community choir is well established or fairly new, programming repertoire that will excite your community choir while staying within their musical limits is one of the biggest challenges a new director will face.

Your program proposal to the board and first concert will make the first and last impression of your artistic vision and values. In my experience in leading community choirs, the board was an excellent resource to ensure that my artistic vision was one that members of the chorus would embrace and the community (audience members) would support while staying within budgetary guidelines. However, one has to be prepared to articulate one's vision and excite the board and chorus about the programming to get significant support. When working with non-auditioned groups, the caveat in considering what to program is that one might either over program or under program. Striking the right balance and having the flexibility to pivot, especially in the early years, is key to success.

Depending on the community choir, they meet once a week and usually have a fall/winter and spring concert, but some may have as many as three concerts. Some collaborate with other organizations or perform with a professional or semi-professional orchestra. All of this should be factored into programming. If the chorus is singing a long masterwork in a season, the masterwork should be their program for that concert with no additional pieces. If the program is a more traditional choral concert, programming an extended work or a shorter masterwork (e.g., Vivaldi's "Gloria") as an anchor piece is very important and it can assist with programming. If you are inclined to program thematically, having a popular work to serve as an anchor may attract an audience depending on the work. Some choose to program the extended work as both their final piece and featured piece. Depending on the nature of the concert, that may or may not be the best way to plan. As a practical matter, an extended work will occupy a significant portion of your concert.

We should plan the length and timing of all choruses, not just community choruses, but community choruses may need to rent venues and include specific contractual limitations. Additionally, planning concerts with an appropriate length is an important consideration. Overprogramming will generally cause fatigue for the choir and audience alike. We may find ourselves in a position where the choir is not prepared, causing anxiety and nerves not only for us but for the choir members. If there are any significant musical issues or a piece is poorly performed, the risk is losing the trust and confidence of chorus and audience.

Underprogramming, on the other hand, is the equivalent to hosting a dinner where the meal is not sufficient to satisfy your guests. If the music is performed at a high level, you can make adjustments to the programming and incorporate more demanding works in the future. A successful concert where the choir seeks out more challenges is not a terrible problem. Losing the trust and confidence of your choir members is a much more serious issue, especially with volunteer community choirs. Underprogramming a high-quality program can actually be an opportunity to challenge your choir in the future by setting aspirational goals, but it should not happen too often. Audiences want to hear a full concert and enjoy the performance; your choristers also do not want to become bored—finding the right balance can be a challenge. But it is better to grow and aspire rather than fail and disappoint.

Directing a community choir can be one of the most exhilarating and musically satisfying experiences a choir director can have. As the director, you have a great deal of freedom to actualize an artistic vision you would not have in other settings. The very nature of community choirs is the community building, which is at the heart of what we do. The members and boards of this group will want you to succeed and will protect you and the organization because they have a long-term investment in the group. Yet directing a community choir in most cases is not a full-time job; working with motivated adults and the freedom to program music for music's sake are a worthwhile experience for any choral conductor.

Notes

1. John Callaway, 2021, "Musings from the Rosenthal Archives of the Chicago Symphony Orchestra Association," from the archives, October 21, https://csoarchives.wordpress.com/tag/wttw/.

2. J. Palkki, 2017, "Inclusivity in Action: Transgender Students in the Choral Classroom," *Choral Journal* (57) 11: 10–34.

3. Steven M. Demorest, Jamey Kelley, and Peter Q. Pfordresher, 2016, "Singing Ability, Musical Self-Concept, and Future Music Participation," *Journal of Research in Music Education* 64 (4): 405–20.

4. Felicity Turner, 2024, "A Day in the Life of Choral Composer Rosephanye Powell," *Stay at Home Choir*. Accessed March 19, 2024, https://stuff.stayathomechoir.com/a-day-in-the-life-of-choral-composer-rosephanye-powell/.

Four

Skill Development and Rehearsal Priorities

Chapter 4 focuses on how to develop choral skills: tone, intonation, breath management, and vowel pronunciation. It also serves as a resource for addressing problems one may encounter when working with a developing ensemble. One common problem is the inability of some members to match pitch. The first section of this chapter is devoted to pitch-matching in children, adolescents, and adults. This chapter will include strategies for advancing a choir from unison singing to singing in harmony. The remainder of the chapter describes exercises to deal with common problems of novice choirs.

"Every child should have the ability to access choral singing through an educational process, so that they can not only learn more about the people around them but perhaps learn a lot more about themselves."

—*Rollo Dilworth*[1]

How many times have we heard someone say, "I can't sing"? Usually, this person is an adult who has held this notion since childhood. They have come to believe that there are those who have "beautiful voices" and those who don't or who are even "tone deaf." Even former Secretary of State and First Lady Hillary Clinton lamented on the presidential campaign trail that a childhood teacher had told her that she couldn't sing, and she believed that to be true well into her adult life. This view of singing puts it in the realm of predestination, like being tall or short or having black hair or brown hair—but singing ability is not an immutable physical attribute.

Singing Is a Teachable and Learnable Skill

As choral educators, we know that singing can be taught. This is why it is offered to nearly all students in elementary and secondary schools. Some singers have an easier time than others with pitch-matching, producing a pleasant tone, and reading music. However, those with more native talent should not be the only ones to receive singing instruction. If reading, writing, and arithmetic were taught only to those possessing natural abilities in these subjects, would this be acceptable on a societal level? On a moral level? Regardless of abilities or limitations of students pursuing any given subject, most are capable of improving skills through study and practice. As musicians, we understand the importance of practice in developing the requisite skills to become accomplished in our field. Applying this philosophy to singing means approaching singing as a skill rather than an activity for the "naturally gifted." Hopefully, this skill is first introduced by the elementary general music teacher and then further developed by the school choral director. In both cases, these professionals serve as voice teachers, and for many they may be the only voice teachers that some singers will have.

The role of choral director/de facto voice teacher is a great responsibility. We are responsible for teaching the care of an instrument that is unique to every individual. Our ability to teach singing effectively and soundly can determine whether the individuals in our ensembles will enjoy a lifetime of singing, have an acceptable or subpar experience, or suffer harm or damage to their instrument. Choral directors must have sound knowledge of vocal technique and the ability to identify harmful habits as many of the singers we encounter will not have the benefit of private voice instruction, save the collegiate music major experience. No matter the range of ages or abilities in a vocal ensemble, a conductor can improve the singing skills of the members by focusing on the following basic elements of good ensemble singing:

- pitch-matching
- posture, breath support, and breath management
- meaningful vocalizations

- vowel unification
- blend, balance, and tone quality
- musical literacy

Pitch-Matching

The ability to match pitch and produce a pleasant tone are basics in the development of a good singer. Most untrained ears are able to discern and identify singing that is "off-key." Research has indicated that pitch-matching ability is critical to one's musical development and self-perception. Moreover, a direct relationship between continued participation in singing and music is tied to pitch-matching ability in the elementary years, particularly for boys.[2] Given that pitch-matching ability is tied to self-perception, choral directors must make the attainment of this skill a top priority, especially for choristers in their formative years. In the middle school years, the voice change in both males and females may cause further complications if these skills have not been mastered earlier. In transgender individuals or those going through gender transition, these issues may be even more complex. Adults struggling with pitch-matching may have a limited range or have trouble connecting sounds they hear with their voice. Many adults I have encountered who struggle with pitch-matching may have not sung in a formal setting during childhood or adolescence. Having access to a quality musical education during childhood and adolescence will give most individuals the opportunity to successfully sing in choral ensembles through adulthood.

Jean Ashworth Bartle has identified children who have difficulties with consistently matching pitch as uncertain singers rather than tone-deaf, which has many negative connotations.[3] Furthermore, the term tone-deaf is disqualifying and often times an inaccurate description. Taken in a very literal way, tone-deaf means that one does not have the ability to hear tones and thus cannot enjoy music of any kind! Similarly, the term monotone has been used to describe individuals who have difficulty in matching pitch. Anyone who has worked with children will understand that most produce a broad range of pitches in their speech, especially during play. Therefore, monotone also fails to identify the true issue. Both terms have been used to exclude individuals from singing in general and choral singing because of the challenges they present to the director and potentially the ensemble. While most choral directors are fully aware that most children are neither tone-deaf nor monotone, the primary concern centers on each singer's ability to consistently match pitch in an appropriate range. Therefore, the term uncertain singer is perhaps the best description for children who may struggle with pitch-matching.

Children may have difficulty consistently matching pitch for a variety of reasons. Some may lack exposure to singing in the home environment, experience developmental delays, come from cultures where singing is reserved for special or specific occasions, or may have physical limitations. Regardless of the challenge that students are experiencing, we must find a way to help them develop singing skills within their abilities. An effective way I have found to help children is through playfulness rather than as a singing instruction task. Using vocal-kinesthetic play could include, for example, having children imitate sounds in nature while physically showing what that sound may look like. Another example is the use of siren sounds for helping students find and connect with their head voice. The best part of these activities is that all children, including those who are not struggling, can participate in this vocal play. The next step is connecting these games to pitch-matching.

Developing Pitch-Matching Skills

The human voice is the best model for children. Every choral conductor should be comfortable in using their own voice to demonstrate foundational singing skills. For those teachers who are cisgender male, falsetto is a useful tool to help children hear and imitate pitches in their own range. Most children may giggle at first when they hear a fully grown cisgender male sing in falsetto. After the initial reaction, falsetto can be an invaluable tool for working with uncertain singers. Eventually, cisgender males and some transgender females should demonstrate their authentic voice. However, children who are in the early stages of vocal development must hear pitches they can produce with their own voice. Additionally, engaging children in vocal exploration and inviting them to connect with you as singers will fortify their trust and bond with you. Cisgender female and some transgender male teachers will naturally have the range that children will be able to match and only need to ensure that they are demonstrating a tone that is appropriate for children. The use of piano should be avoided if possible as the timbre of the instrument does not match the sound of a human voice and its percussive nature does not promote the technique we would want our singers to develop. The piano is a good reference for pitch, but a poor model for vocal tone.

Working with Struggling Singers

Despite our best efforts to guide children and adults in the development of pitch-matching skills, some still may struggle. If singers demonstrate little or no improvement over time, then we must find additional ways to provide the support they require. Working with small groups, of mixed ability, when possible, is one potential approach. Depending on the severity of the challenges, it may be more appropriate to work with individual singers if we have a clear strategy and can provide instruction discretely.

Small group work with mixed-ability singers can sometimes help struggling individuals as well as individuals who easily excel at pitch-matching. In this setting, the struggling individual will have age-appropriate models surrounding them, and the others who are not struggling may develop leadership skills. It is important to avoid placing all the struggling individuals, particularly children, in "pull-out" lessons as this can invite a degree of marginalization and demoralization within the group. Although it may seem practical to group these children together, it may create an emotional experience that leaves them thinking that they "can't sing," "shouldn't sing," or are just untalented.

Individual assistance can be the most effective way of helping our uncertain singers, but it can also stigmatize them if we do not approach it in a purposeful and discreet way. If we make the decision to work with a singer individually, we should make that opportunity available to others, including those that are not struggling. When we make the decision to offer individualized assistance, we should ask ourselves:

- Who needs this help?
- How can I work with the student in a way that does not single them out?
- What are the specific skills that will be addressed?
- Am I trying to help with accessing head voice?
- Am I trying to help with placement/control that is causing pitch issues?
- Am I testing to see if they can match any pitches purposefully?

Once we have considered these issues, then we must have a strategy to address and follow-up on each issue. We should also provide exercises for the child to do on their own to strengthen their skills.

Pitch-Matching in Adolescence

Adolescence can be a very challenging time for most individuals. As children grow into teenagers, their interests become more focused, and they tend to gravitate toward those activities where they feel successful. As middle school begins, students often are presented with the choice of participating in ensembles or pursuing other issues. The activities they select reflect and define their identity. As such, we may assume that students in a choral ensemble in middle school or high school have made the choice to be there. However, in some cases, students may have been placed into a choral ensemble by the school administration or through their parents insisting that they join.

Regardless of how students arrive in our ensembles, we are responsible for ensuring that we provide them with the very best instruction we can offer. Individuals who are enthusiastic about joining our ensemble likely have had positive previous experiences with singing. They may already have a healthy musical self-image to serve as a foundation for their future growth. These circumstances do not mean that they will be immune to pitch-matching issues. However, their previous experiences and positive attitudes do suggest that they will likely feel more secure and be willing to take risks in their learning. Singers who join our ensemble at the request of parents or due to scheduling issues beyond their control may have a harder time. Despite students' level of experience or comfort as singers, we must be aware that heightened self-consciousness will be a factor and can manifest itself in many forms. If we are working with preteens or teenagers who are unsure about singing or who hold a hostile attitude toward singing, then we must first work to gain their trust.

This is especially true of male singers. Tenors and basses in middle and high school ensembles tend to be in the minority. If they have had singing experience in the past, they will undoubtedly be more confident than their first-time singing peers. This confidence, however, may be affected when they start experiencing voice change and the range limitation that comes with it. In fact, they may once again experience difficulty with matching pitch. This difficulty may arise due to voice change, but it can also be brought about through the selection of literature.

Choral Literature and Pitch-Matching

During adolescence, especially during the middle school years, it is important to consider the range and tessitura when selecting music. If the range or tessitura of your chosen literature is not well-matched to your singers, they will suffer pitch problems not specifically linked to their pitch-matching ability. As choral directors we must be flexible and know how and what to program music that will allow our singers to succeed. Think outside of the box. Soprano, Alto, Baritone (SAB) literature is an option for middle school/junior high school choirs that many rely upon. Oftentimes, it is not the most suitable choice. Some composers and arrangers of this literature may assume that all boys have the same range (and sometimes a range that goes very low). Some directors will assign changing voices or unchanged voices to the "baritone" part regardless of their range. The singing results often in non-chord tones that suggest pitch-matching issues. But pitch is not necessarily the problem. Imagine an orchestra assigning a violin player the cello or double bass part on their instrument! Most would agree that such a move would be ludicrous, yet some in our profession believe that a comparable approach is acceptable for our young adolescent singers. Three-part mixed music, limited-range music, and music designed for the changing voice is a more thoughtful way to approach this period of vocal transition. Whatever our approach to finding success for young adolescent singers, the first step is to find options that will allow them to sing a part that they physically can sing. In some cases, we may have to create the part for them or rearrange parts based on their range at a given point in time. Our knowledge of theory, voice leading, and chord structure could come in handy in this case. It is more important to achieve that success even if that means that we carefully modify parts.

Once we are certain we have chosen appropriate literature, assigned our adolescent singers the correct part, and that literature is not the cause of pitch-matching difficulties, then it is likely that the pitch-matching difficulty is related to inexperience or lack of exposure to using a full range. For example, some singers in popular genres sing in a limited range (often in the alto/high tenor range), and our adolescent singers may try to emulate that style even though that may not be their actual range or where their voice naturally sits. Whatever the case may be, we must find a comfortable range and tessitura for them where they can consistently match pitch. Games and such may still be effective, but they should be age appropriate. Kinesthetic approaches should continue to be incorporated as much as possible and should also be age appropriate.

Pitch-Matching and Cisgender Male Singers

As mentioned earlier, the choral conductor must be comfortable with vocal modeling. Some studies suggest that those who struggle with singing are best served by a human model.[4] However, during adolescence, particularly when working with lower voices, the choral director may or may not be able to serve as a vocal model for all voice types. Cisgender males and transgender females (prior to hormone therapy) may have the use of falsetto and may be able to demonstrate in multiple octaves. However, cisgender female conductors, in most cases, will not have the lower octave range. Therefore, some cisgender female conductors may not have the adequate range to demonstrate in the octave of their cisgender male students. In this case, the piano can assist with pitch-matching, despite its limitations.

Upon hearing the speaking voice of our cisgender male students, it usually becomes apparent where their natural tessitura is. Most boys will naturally sing in the octave that is comfortable for them. The conductor should encourage their students to sing in a comfortable octave when working on pitch-matching skills and then work to expand the range and find ways to help their singers access different registers of their voice, including falsetto. Positive reinforcement of pitch-matching in a comfortable octave should be a priority for singers who have not been able to match pitch consistently. Moreover, speaking with our singers when they are not matching pitch is important. If they are not aware, helping them improve their attention to this skill without causing them shame or embarrassment is critical to their future enjoyment of singing. Simply ignoring pitch-matching issues and allowing students to sing off pitch without remedy or plan of action is a disservice to them and the other singers of the ensemble. Cisgender males go through a rather dramatic voice change in some cases, but they should have the opportunity to have a meaningful experience in a choral ensemble.

Pitch-Matching and Cisgender Female Singers

Cisgender adolescent females tend to have fewer issues with pitch-matching, and choral directors deal with other vocal issues during this period. In the case of adolescent cisgender female singers, pitch-matching issues may be related to speaking and/or singing consistently in chest voice, which may or may not be related to their voice changes. If this is the case, it would be wise to explore head voice sounds before actual pitch. The conductor should demonstrate what those sounds are and ask their singers to emulate these sounds. Once it is apparent that the singers can emulate these sounds, then the conductor can try to connect them with specific pitches. While building the upper range and developing pitch-matching in both head voice and middle voice, the conductor should avoid programming music that is in a low tessitura. The conductor should also be mindful of the timbre and mix throughout the low and middle voice. In the case of transgender and gender-neutral students, many factors can affect pitch-matching ability and skill. Hormone therapy, transition stage, and emotional/psychological comfort may be factors in addition to the factors that may contribute to pitch-matching difficulties in their cisgender counterparts. Additionally, some students would like to keep both a male- and female-sounding voice while others want to leave the old voice behind.[5] Above all else, addressing pitch-matching for singers during adolescence must be done in a manner that creates a psychologically and emotionally safe environment while simultaneously addressing their physiological strengths and limitations.

Pitch-Matching and Adults

Some individuals decide to join a chorus later in life but have never sung in one or had access to music instruction in their formative years. Some may have begun formal music instruction during or after puberty and may struggle with matching pitch. Some studies suggest that an estimated 10 to 15 percent of the adults of the Western population sings "out-of-tune."[6] If pitch-matching for an individual in an ensemble is inconsistent, even if the voice has the potential for exceptional timbre or already has demonstrated beautiful tone, the singer may lack the confidence to fully participate in a choral ensemble. A pleasing vocal timbre is fully appreciated only if the singer has developed the skill to match pitch consistently. Through a humanistic, systematic, and realistic approach, the choral director can help these individuals enjoy a lifetime of singing.

To make this improvement a reality, the music teacher or conductor must be committed to helping these individuals without drawing undue attention to them. One of the first steps is finding their comfortable range. When working with adults who have volunteered their time to participate in an ensemble, there is a fair level of intrinsic motivation as well as peer support to ameliorate some challenges that they may have. Adult volunteers want to sing, and many are aware of their vocal issues. In fact, some join our ensembles to seek help with these issues and hope to grow vocally as well as be part of a community. Some individuals may have had an interest in singing in childhood and/or adolescence and may have not found a patient or welcoming ensemble to join. It is possible for adults who have been told that they "can't sing" or to "mouth the words" when they were a child because they had pitch issues to revisit singing. A community choir and/or church choir may be the place for them to enjoy choir singing even if they do not consistently match pitch.

If the ensemble is large enough, these singers can be placed next to stronger singers or section leaders who will be able to assist them on their journey. Research suggests that live vocal stimulus can assist singers with difficulties of pitch and is more effective than the piano.[7] However, the progress of adult singers with pitch-matching difficulties will vary. If we check in with them as well as their peers discreetly, they will undoubtedly make progress and have a meaningful experience. Additionally, if we discuss parts of their range where they consistently match pitch and other parts of their range where they struggle, we can encourage them to sing what is comfortable and positively reinforce what is successful. In terms of where they struggle, we can delicately let them know that certain parts of their range have not yet developed. If we are honest and positive with adults, they will appreciate it and will try their best to contribute to the ensemble even if they struggle with pitch-matching. Moreover, they will have a place where they not only belong but will become some of the most invested individuals in the ensemble.

Breath Support, Breath Management, and Posture

Although pitch-matching is a critical component of singing skill, tone and timbre are also important in the development of singing technique. While directors may believe that tone quality is innate and therefore cannot be improved upon, most seasoned choral directors know that singers can attain a pleasant tone (by Western standards) by honing particular vocal skills. The development of tone within an ensemble requires the conductor to understand and to communicate basic concepts of tone production. Unlike instrumental conductors, most choral directors must teach their ensembles how to use their instruments. The conductor must teach appropriate posture for standing and sitting, explain and reinforce concepts of breath support, and both describe and demonstrate the phonation of vowels that will result in appropriate tone for the genre being performed.

Posture

Posture is one of the building blocks for adequate breath support. We breathe every day without making an ordeal of it, but proper singing posture must be taught in a systematic way so that it becomes a habit. Moreover, we must teach appropriate posture for sitting and standing positions in order to have proper breath support.

The three postures I use with ensembles are standing, seated, and relaxed (an acceptable posture when singers are not singing). These postures are summarized in table 4.1.

Standing posture should not be too relaxed or tense but requires the singer to have an elevated sternum, hands at their sides, and a level head position (where the larynx is comfortably low but not pressed down). Seated posture should begin with establishing standing posture as the default position. Unless chorus members have chairs specifically designed for posture, singers should not sit back in their chairs when singing. Ideally, singers should be able to stand easily from a seated position without much

Table 4.1	Choral Singing Postures
Standing Posture	Feet shoulder-width apart, elevated sternum, hands at sides or holding folders at upper ribcage height, head level, attentive demeanor
Seated Postured	Sitting forward on chair, feet on floor (if they reach), elevated sternum, hands resting on thighs or holding folder at upper ribcage height, head level, attentive demeanor.
Relaxed Posture	Casual posture, relaxed. May be used during either sitting or standing when the choir is not singing.

change in the torso. In the case of older adult singers, they may not be able to make these adjustments so easily. Some may have physical limitations that may prevent them from having "ideal" posture for singing. When this is the case, I ask them to do the best they can, given their physical limitations. If the singers are able, I ask them to sit at the edge of their chairs and practice standing from this position. In teaching posture, as well as any other aspect of technique, I reinforce these habits in each rehearsal, especially when working with an inexperienced group. With younger singers, I spend a few minutes of each rehearsal making a game out of practicing these stances. From a psychological perspective, posture also can be used for classroom management and for focusing the group to achieve a rehearsal/performance mindset. Once posture has been established as the foundation for teaching good breath support, we can address the fundamentals of breathing.

Breath as the Foundation of Tone

Breath support and breath management are the building blocks of tone development. The concepts of breath support and breath management can be difficult to teach in a group setting. Choral conductors with extensive training in singing and vocal pedagogy may have been taught the technique of appoggio. As explained by Richard Miller in *The Structure of Singing*:[8]

> In appoggio technique, the sternum must initially find a moderately high position; this position is then retained throughout the inspiration-expiration cycle. Shoulders are relaxed, but the sternum never slumps. Because the ribs are attached to the sternum, sternal posture in part determines diaphragmatic position. If the sternum lowers, the ribs cannot maintain an expanded position, and the diaphragm must ascend more rapidly. Both the epigastric and umbilical regions should be stabilized so that a feeling of internal-external muscular balance is present. This sensation directly influences the diaphragm. (1986, p. 24)

You may read this quote and wonder: How can I translate that into something meaningful to a large ensemble? Donald Neuen's *Choral Concepts*[9] explains the teaching process in this way:

> When teaching breathing to ensembles, do so in a manner that will be completely understood and easily applied by each individual. The directives must be easy and obvious, nothing complicated or hard to envision. To tell the chorus members that they must now begin to expand, to inhale and contract, to exhale, and then expect them to do it, is unreasonable and practically impossible. (2002, p. 18)

Enabling singers to experience the conditions that promote adequate breath support is really the most effective way to instill the concept rather than lecturing them on these concepts. One method that has worked well for my ensembles is to instruct the choristers to stretch both arms straight up over their heads, hold that position for a moment, and then slowly lower both arms to their sides while keeping the sternum in the same position it was in when the arms were raised. This puts the neck, shoulders, and sternum in the proper alignment for expanding the ribs to allow optimum intake of breath and for abdominal muscles to provide support for expelling the breath.

Developing the Breath

Finding exercises to teach breathing without phonation can be a challenge. Not all exercises are suitable for everyone, and some could lead to unintended consequences. Conductors should keep a watchful eye as choristers do breathing exercises. I have encountered ambitious students who, wishing to please, go beyond what is necessary, setting themselves up for developing bad habits, such as stuffing air or creating too much subglottic pressure. Breathing exercises that I have found to work universally require the singer to breathe in an efficient manner. If you ask a choir to inhale and their shoulders rise and their breath is audible, this is a sign the breathing is inefficient, and posture should be reexamined. If the majority of the choir is giving the appearance of low breathing and the breath is inaudible, you can have the singers practice breath management and breathing exercises without phonation. It is important to encourage good habits; teach singers to be self-aware as well as encourage them to be independent to the point where they begin to self-correct without your assistance. If we can do this, our singers will be able to develop the necessary skills to become more independent.

> Breathing could be considered the cornerstone of all good rehearsal technique. Breathing by the conductor for and with the ensemble is of central importance. A lack of breath will sabotage any rehearsal technique and cause numerous musical missteps. With every inhalation, we are confronted with an opportunity to initiate and birth musical line. It must also be understood that we habituate the cycle of things both good and bad by how we breathe.[10]

Breath management can be a perplexing concept. Many singers hearing the term breath control make every effort to "control their breath," often to the detriment of their singing. I prefer the term breath management because it is more accurate. In my experience, singers find the idea of management a more organic approach to breathing. While there are no perfect exercises for inducing good breath management practices, some exercises may help choristers think about how to manage their breath for various durations. The director must be aware of each member of the ensemble for any exercise to be effective. Table 4.2 highlights a few basic exercises I have found to be effective and easy to monitor with small or large ensembles at any level, including beginning choirs.

These simple exercises are four of many that may be taught. Exercises should be customized to fit the ensemble and the conductor. Other useful methods of making singers aware of breath management include having singers lean forward against a wall (used to induce lower breathing and ensure that the shoulders are not raised upon inhalation) or having

54   Chapter Four

singers place a book on their stomach at home while lying down, and so forth. Whatever one's exercise of choice, it should draw attention to efficient breathing, engage singers in a meaningful way, and create healthy habits. Most importantly, exercises should never be done on "auto-pilot."

Table 4.2 Breath Management Exercises	
Four and Twenty	Singers inhale for four beats and expel the air on an [s] for twenty beats. The speed of the exercise can be increased or the number of beats for exhaling. Incorporating *ritardando* at the end will encourage good breath support at the end of phrases that may be long or *ritard*. This exercise may also be performed on f or ʃ.
Pulsed "F"	Have ensemble members place their hands below the rib cage; inhale and exhale while making a f sound. Singers should breathe between each f. Repeat at least four times: *f–f–f–f*. Direct the singers' attention to the sensation they feel. The conductor should be scanning the room and listening to ensure the ensemble members are in the best posture and are breathing efficiently.
Extended [u]	Have ensemble member sing a [u] vowel at a *mp* or *mf* dynamic. Singers can sustain for ten, fifteen, and twenty beats.
Extended Phrases: Connecting Breath Management to Music	Choose a passage within the music you have programmed with a particularly long phrase and have the entire choir sing the phrase. • The dynamic of the phrase should be stated. • Stagger breathing should not be used; singers should be encouraged to manage their breath to make it to the end of the phrase. • Monitor the quality of sound.

Conductors must remain actively engaged in observing their ensembles throughout the rehearsal and, if necessary, occasionally reminding singers how techniques from one of the exercises can be applied to what they are rehearsing.

Meaningful Vocalization

Most choral directors do some kind of warm-up activity with their ensembles prior to singing choral literature. Sometimes these activities are done merely out of routine. This may not be the best way to capitalize on the fresh energy and focus that an ensemble brings at the beginning of a rehearsal. Our time is valuable. More importantly, our singers' time is valuable, and they need to have a meaningful experience when they sing in our rehearsals.

The choral rehearsal must begin with purpose. I prefer to use the term vocalize and to use intentional vocalizations to improve the singers' skill level. The vocalization period is the principal time choral conductors can focus exclusively on singing technique and choral tone. Therefore, planning effective vocalizations that build on skills, whether musical or vocal skills, can only help our choirs improve.

Vocalizations are beneficial only if the conductor has a purpose for them and is actively listening to the singers and assessing their progress. Conductors should be able to explain in clear terms to their singers why they are asking them to perform vocal exercises. Moreover, it should be obvious to more accomplished singers what purpose the exercises serve, and the singers should be able to eventually explain why a particular vocalization is being used and what skill is being honed.

Vocalizations should be appropriate for the age, experience level, and size of the ensemble. They serve to establish the sound expectations for the ensemble. If the ensemble consists of novice singers, exercises and expectations would vary from those practiced with a more seasoned choir. A small, less experienced choir may not sing confidently because the individual members of the group may feel exposed as they sing. An ensemble of this nature may need simple exercises that focus on pure vowel production

Table 4.3 Building Sonic Unity	
Siren	Model an emergency vehicle siren and invite singers to echo. Begin with narrow range and expand to cover full range. Start in the lower part of the head voice, arc to the top of the range, and glissando downward into the lower range.
Lip Trills	Have singers use "brr" to imitate the action of a lawnmower or boat engine on pitch. Explore the various ranges on specific pitches.
5-4-3-2-1	Sing from *sol* downward to *do* on "u" and other vowels. Begin in the midrange and work toward the outer bounds of the singers' range.
Messa-di-voce	This exercise should be performed in unison. Vowel matching should be a priority as well as quality of sound across vowels and dynamic levels. The exercise should begin at *piano*, crescendo to *forte*, and decrescendo back to *piano*. i-e-a-o-u $p < f > p$
See the Rich Tone exercise from *Sing Legato!** See example in figure 4.1.	

Note

* Kenneth Jennings, 1982, *Sing Legato!* (San Diego, CA: Kjos Music Company).

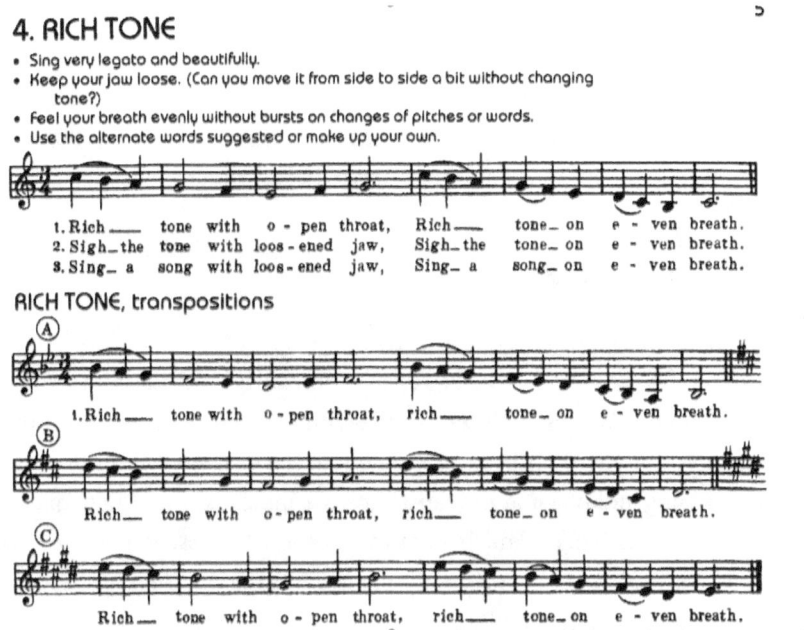

Figure 4.1 From *Sing Legato!* by Kenneth Jennings, published by Neil A. Kjos Music Company in 1982.

and blend. Producing these sounds creates a sense of unity—a strength in sound that feels greater than the number of people in the ensemble. Singing in this sound builds the confidence of each member of the ensemble, and the group's sound will be vibrant and alive. Exercises to create this sound are shown in table 4.3.

The siren enables singers to connect their breath to head voice and use their full register. Lip trills are another tactic for connecting breath to pitch without using a specific vowel and without putting undue strain on the vocal folds. Lip trills post-COVID may not be widely used in a group setting but we can demonstrate and encourage our singers to practice this exercise on their own. When using pitch with vowels, a descending 5-4-3-2-1 (sol-fa-mi-re-do) exercise on "u" (and other vowels) in the middle of the range may be a good starting point. Vocalizations should not start in extreme registers of the voice. For treble voices, begin 5-4-3-2-1 exercises about an octave above middle C, at A or B♭ for mixed voices, then descend or ascend by whole steps. When adding vowels to the exercises, we must be aware of the regional accents within our ensemble, preconceived notions of tone production, and innate ability to access head voice.

Vowel Unification

Vowel unification—in other words, having singers match vowels across vocal parts and registers—is the key to achieving blend and assisting a choir to sing in tune. Working with the vocalization process, we must instill the fundamentals of vowel unification throughout the ensemble. For our singers to fully sing and blend at the same time, we must insist that they match vowels when vocalizing. If, during the vocalization process, you notice that the vowels are not being consistently matched in the middle register, it is important to call the ensemble's attention to it. Tell the singers what sound was produced and offer a solution for correcting it. Allowing our ensembles to sing with vowels and tone during vocalizations may not be appropriate for the genres they are performing. By not prioritizing vowel production/unification, we are simply warming-up or even worse: practicing bad habits. Choral voice builders, such as the late Frauke Haasemann, would often re-vocalize a group when changing styles or genres. Vocalizations and teaching vocal technique may be helpful at other times than the beginning of the rehearsal. However, purposeful vocalizations will reinforce the habits we would like our choirs to develop. Remember: practice makes permanent!

The International Phonetic Alphabet (IPA) is a valuable tool for any choral conductor for teaching correct vowel production, though many have not had exposure to it in their undergraduate or graduate education. Although we may not have the time to teach IPA and it may not be appropriate to teach it to all our ensembles, we must be able to model and explain in very clear language the vowels we wish to hear. We can teach very basic IPA vowels that give our ensemble a specific sense of vowels we want them to produce, which is feasible if we teach in a school setting where we regularly meet with our choirs. However, church and community choirs may not have the time to explore the nuances of IPA and modeling, and explaining vowel production would be the most practical way of unifying vowel production and quality. In addition to vowel quality, time allotted to vocalization should also include strategies for addressing diphthongs, vowel modification, and basic vocal technique. Each of these matters can be addressed before facing these challenges in choral literature.

Blend and Balance

Many choral giants of the past and present (Weston Noble, Robert Fountain, Robert Shaw, Charles Bruffy, and André Thomas, to name a few) have used various methods to achieve blend and balance. However, when we work with less experienced choirs, subscribing to any one philosophy may not be as easy or effective initially. Some choral directors prioritize achieving perfect blend while others prefer a more robust sound. For example, some conductors of non-academic ensembles may select choristers with smaller, less colorful voices and exclude singers with larger, more robust voices from their ensembles. While others look for more soloistic operatic voices to join their choirs. There are several historic schools of singing in the United States that address blend and balance (table 4.4). Harold Swan[11] cites six choral schools of thought in his *Choral Conducting: A Symposium*. This is a short summary and is not a full or extensive description of these choral schools of thought, or an endorsement of any one school.

    As stated earlier, there are many philosophies in how to achieve choral tone and balance. Robert Fountain believed that both solo and choral-oriented singers could sing in the same choir. The Oberlin College Choir as well as Fountain's choirs at the University of Wisconsin–Madison were well known for their contributions to choral music in the United States. Many choral directors borrow from various philosophies to achieve blend and balance. Subscribing to one school over another or integrating various schools into one's approach is the prerogative of each director. I believe proper balance and blend in an ensemble can be facilitated by placing similar voices together within the ensemble. In order to identify vocal timbres and position singers to enhance our sound, I have to hear each individual

Table 4.4 Historic Choral Schools	
School	*Philosophy and Characteristics*
John Finley Williamson Westminster Choir Sound	1. Vitality of tone. 2. Dark full-bodied vibrant sound. 3. Each singer should develop as a musician. 4. Differences of vocal timbres are recognized. 5. Vowel modification and balance taught by a series of rules.
Father William J. Finn— Paulist Choristers	1. Beauty of tone. 2. Tone is small, bright, floating tone. 3. Chorophony—the chorister's tone is like the color of an orchestral instrument. 4. Vowels will be used to imitate timbres of instruments for example [i] is for string and [u] is for flute. 5. All vocalization will affect tone color.
F. Melius Christiansen— St. Olaf Choir	1. Good ensemble quality exists only as individual concepts disappear. 2. Solo vibrato is discouraged. 3. Tone is perfectly blended and individual voices do not stand out. 4. Unison singing with an emphasis of vowel matching, modification of tone. 5. Emphasis on singing on the vowels and locking chords.
Fred Waring, The Pennsylvanians (Glee Club)	1. Diction is used to achieve balance and unity. 2. Excellent diction and comfortable tone. 3. All sounds have a slot in time. 4. Exaggeration of vowel sounds and consonants with pitched duration. 5. Rhythm is paramount.
John C. Wilcox, Joseph Klein, and Douglas Stanley	1. Singing is scientific. 2. Emphasis on each individual improving their vocal technique through the lens of solo singing. 3. The tone is vibrant, vital, and operatic. 4. The development of a clear natural vibrato is encouraged. 5. Essentially a chorus of soloists.

School	Philosophy and Characteristics
Robert Shaw	1. Integrity of choral tone. 2. Vigorous tone and elasticity in tone. Precision in phrasing and diction. 3. Music is order in sound: pitch, tone, dynamics, speech, and rhythm. 4. Count sing is a common technique to achieve precision and blend. 5. Singers are placed carefully.

confidently sing a five-note descending scale in a comfortable part of their range. Based on what I hear, I position singers within the ensemble so that voices with a lighter quality are toward the ends and front of the ensemble while large voices with dark qualities are toward the center and back. While this process can be time consuming, I have found it worthwhile as it allows me to achieve the best blend possible with large and diverse ensembles. This method of voicing in my experience also allows the singers to sing as naturally as possible. Although this process works well with a larger ensemble, it may be more challenging with smaller ones unless the voices are similar. Therefore, I am willing to sacrifice blend to an extent, especially with developing singers, if it means the singers will sing with a healthier, more vibrant sound in the long run.

Notational Literacy

Many in our field would agree that the development of musically literate choristers is important. Yet musical literacy has many components. The skills and literacies singers need to be informed performers include elements of history, culture (race, religion, gender), emotional awareness, and aural and notation skills. Often, singers are not treated as "real musicians" because they are unable to read music. How many times have we heard the phrase singers and musicians as if singers were not musicians because they did not play an instrument? Some singers may have a more comprehensive knowledge of the music they are performing than some instrumentalists.

However, teaching notational literacy in our profession may not be a high priority for everyone in our profession. Many other skills and literacies can be shared from the podium, but choir leaders often wrestle with aural/notational literacies.

Expectations for the level an ensemble should attain in aural/notational literacies differ depending on the ages and abilities of the singers and the type of ensemble. A community choir, for instance, may not prioritize notational literacy because their mission and function does not require it for participation. School ensembles, however, are another matter. In many high schools and middle schools, chorus is part of an established curriculum. The conductor of a school chorus is a music educator first and foremost. Educators in, say, language arts or a foreign language are expected to teach students to read and write in that language and to comprehend the cultural context of what they read. Yet the pressure on music educators to stage successful public performances can be a barrier to teaching aural/notational and other literacies.

Those who do not understand techniques of developing functionally literate singers may think that notational literacy occurs by osmosis simply by performing the music or having sheet music available to them. The ability to identify musical symbols does not necessarily constitute functional literacy. To draw an analogy, to be considered literate in a spoken language, one must be able to minimally read and write in that language. This section is not a comprehensive guide to the teaching of reading and writing music but is intended to give basic tools for beginning the process of teaching these skills to chorus members.

The teacher must choose a musical lexicon and be consistent with that choice. Some choose numbers, note names, or solfège. My preferred system is solfège using moveable "do"- and "la"-based minor and incorporating Curwen hand signs; other methods use numbers to teach pitch reading as most singers can count to seven. For teaching rhythm, I find Kodály effective for early success, but for the long term, teaching one's singers how to count is ideal. I also have seen choral educators use other systems with success. These include TAKADIMI, Gordon method, and Dalcroze, to name a few. Whatever system you choose, be consistent, committed, and flexible enough to change if it does not work for you or your students.

Once you select a system, teach it to the chorus members and work on ear training before asking the singers to use the system in reading musical notation. Ear training exercises at the beginning of rehearsal can be combined with asking the singers to read the pitches. This process should be systematic and done at each rehearsal, especially if the singers are musically inexperienced. With younger singers, making a game of it can be very effective. By developing the ear consistently, fluency in the chosen musical lexicon develops as well, thus preparing the ear for challenges that may be encountered in written notation. As with any educational activity in which we are building skills, this effective scaffolding gives students the necessary support to develop musical and vocal skills. Chapter 5 includes samples of simple sight-reading exercises for beginning ensembles as well as how to incorporate ear training and develop musical fluency.

In each rehearsal, the skills being developed should be connected to written notation. For a novice group, the exercises used to teach notation will be easier than any of the ear training exercises prior to looking at notation. Begin teaching reading notation by limiting how much notation is initially introduced. A fundamental component of teaching note reading successfully is that it should be simple enough for choristers to experience success and that it uses information students are already familiar with. If the exercises are too complex, choristers may become discouraged. If they are too simple, you can move to more complex reading exercises.

The most important aspect about teaching note reading (or anything for that matter) is to make sure the students are in flow. When our students are in flow, they are challenged and can grow but are not burdened to the point of frustration or bored because they are not sufficiently challenged. Over time, we can and should ask our students to create their own exercises with the knowledge they have. When we do this, we must be very clear in the parameters we set. When asking our students to compose exercises, it would be wise to have them do so as a class, then in a small group setting, and finally individually. This section barely scratches the surface of what it means to be musically literate. Its intent is to provide guidance in developing a strategy to address the most basic components of music literacy that should be part of any music education setting.

Rehearsal Priorities

Rehearsal priorities should command as much consideration in a choral conductor's duties as teaching vocal technique. The following rehearsal priorities are based on the rehearsal hierarchies of André Thomas,[12] retired professor from Florida State University and visiting professor of choral conducting (2020–2021) at Yale University, and artist associate for the London Symphony Orchestra.

For the members of an ensemble to bring a composition to life, accuracy of rhythms and pitches must be a top priority. As choral directors, the teaching of accurate rhythms and pitches is perhaps more our responsibility than that of instrumental conductors who ask their players to practice the correct pitches on their instrument without another instrument of reference. Most of our singers do not have absolute or perfect pitch, and many do not play instruments typically used as a pitch reference. Unless we are working with a highly elite ensemble, we should expect to help our singers learn notes and rhythms. If we do not have the luxury of a rehearsal accompanist, we must apply the necessary skills to sing all parts as well as to play parts on the piano (in addition to teaching our singers to decode notation). A conductor who fails to ensure correct rhythms and pitches from the outset will inevitably have to battle with choristers unlearning incorrect rhythms and pitches. It is better to never have learned something than to learn something incorrectly and have the challenge of undoing a bad habit. Furthermore, prioritizing accurate rhythms and pitches is the first step in honoring a composer's intentions.

The next step is requiring singers to perform with an appropriate tone and use vowels suitable for the style of the piece being rehearsed, which also helps stabilize the ensemble's intonation. Conductors of novice ensembles should focus on teaching head tone and developing a free sound based on a solid concept of vowels. Teaching our singers to match vowels and to access all registers are important skills for all vocal ensembles and styles in most cases. However, sound concepts are defined by the songs being sung, and conductors will need to guide choirs in matching song style. As the ensemble advances, we can develop different tone colors appropriate for specific styles and modify vowels and tone.

Similarly, diction and articulation as well as the correct pronunciation of text are critical to producing a quality performance of a work. What exactly is the point of setting text to music if listeners can't discern the words? The acoustics of the performance space will influence the approach to diction and articulation, but this consideration follows the attention given to language. A conductor must understand the mechanics of the language in which the ensemble is performing. Many languages have different pronunciation rules for speaking and singing. Conductors should make every effort to become aware of these rules. If the piece is in a language foreign to the ensemble, the advice of a native speaker should be sought. The conductor might begin by studying a pronunciation guide and then speaking the text in posing questions to the expert for feedback. If possible, invite the expert to model for, listen to, and provide feedback to the ensemble. It may also be helpful to obtain a recording of the accurate pronunciation of the text for ongoing reference. Precision in pronunciation and enunciation will elevate the quality of the ensemble.

Attention to precision cannot be limited to pronunciation of text. Broad precision is a hallmark of the greatest ensembles. Even in the earliest stages of learning a piece, the conductor should give the ensemble tools and rules for developing precision. These tools include placing ending consonants on rests (when applicable) and shortening notes at the ends of phrases to ensure adequate breath intake for a precise entrance on the next phrase. Teaching these norms at the initial learning stages of a piece reduces later struggles to polish and unify the ensemble. Another effective tool, a staple of the late Robert Shaw, is count-singing. Not only does count-singing improve an ensemble's precision, but it is also the best way for choristers to decipher a complex or unusual rhythm. A novice ensemble lacking strong notational literacy skills may regard count-singing as more of a frustration than a help, making this method a challenge to teach. To avoid frustration and establish count-singing as an important tool of musicianship, it should first be taught in isolated homophonic passages.

Rhythmic perfection, pitch accuracy, and precise diction mean little without phrasing and expression for evoking the emotional immediacy of vocal music. Word stress and punctuation can, and should, help guide phrasing choices. Expressive choices should be made from a historically informed perspective. Renaissance, Baroque, Classical, Romantic, and modern choral music and the composers of these respective musical eras have expressive devices, harmonic language, and musical norms specific to their period of history. Additionally, the country, culture, and original language of the piece inform how that piece should be sung. If performing a composition not in the original language, the phrasing based on language may require further study. Do not assume that the English text is a literal translation or even an accurate paraphrasing of the original text. Try to determine if the rise and fall of the line in the original language matches the English text. Whenever possible, compositions should be performed in their original language. Understanding the marriage between musical writing and text should inform all interpretive musical decisions, including how to determine appropriate dynamic contrasts.

Part of music's magic resides in the affective use of dynamic intensities. The conductor must determine the appropriate dynamics within both a piece and the ensemble. In early music, like music from the Renaissance and Baroque eras, dynamic contrast may not be explicit within the score. In this case, the conductor must evaluate the texture and performance norms of the time period in which the piece was written. Contrapuntal music will require discerning which lines to bring out dynamically and which should be subdued. When the composer is explicit with dynamic markings, it is the responsibility of the conductor to observe those dynamics and insist that the ensemble do so. When preparing a score, color coding or some other method of marking dynamic contrasts can help draw your attention to them. You should also be aware that phrase motion can imply dynamic contrasts. Dynamics within the ensemble should also depend upon their impact on the blend and balance of the ensemble.

Blend and balance are often linked to the ensemble's personnel and the conductor's literature choices. Blend can be achieved in many ways, as discussed earlier in this chapter. In some schools of thought, blending requires voices to sing with as little character as possible to achieve blend. In certain styles of music, adult females will be asked to sound like prepubescent children—senza vibrato. When working with novice ensembles, asking for blend by employing these strategies may cause singers to develop vocal problems which will negatively affect their sound and intonation.

Balance within an ensemble affects how blend is perceived. Many choral ensembles have more treble voices than tenors and basses. Such ensembles can achieve a balanced sound with carefully chosen literature that organically allows for balance. For an ensemble with very few bass clef voices, the conductor should select literature that keeps these singers on the same part when possible. In cases with too few bass clef voices to balance the treble voices, creative three-part solutions should be explored. When we select literature, it is important to ensure that we have a balanced ensemble to perform the work to truly honor the composer's intent.

If singing requires the teaching of skills in place of innate talent, then we must develop strategies to teach these skills. One of the fundamental skills singers must develop at a fairly early age is the ability to match pitch. In this chapter, we have considered the importance of developing singers' skills in matching pitch, as well as other skills singers need to be successful. Through teaching basic singing technique and developing specific choral skills such as vowel unification, blend, balance, and tone quality, we can enhance the majority of novice choirs over time. Regardless of the choir we are working with, each of these skills should be given a great deal of consideration in both our daily planning and long-term planning as choral directors. In a school setting, we must teach notational literacy. Depending on the choirs we work with and their mission, teaching notational literacy and broader musical literacy is worthwhile. In each rehearsal, season, and year, we should ponder the following: What kind of experience am I giving my singers? Are they growing as a whole? Is each individual growing?

Notes

1. Brendan Lyons, 2017, "Page 28." *Cued In*, July 19, https://blogs.jwpepper.com/page/28/?p=1662.

2. Steven M. Demorest, Jamey Kelley, and Peter Q. Pfordresher, 2016, "Singing Ability, Musical Self-Concept, and Future Music Participation," *Journal of Research in Music Education* 64 (4): 405–20.

3. Jean Ashworth Bartle, 1993, *Lifeline for Children's Choir Directors* (New York: Alfred Music).

4. Roni Y. Granot, Rona Israel-Kolatt, Avi Gilboa, and Tsafrir Kolatt, 2013, "Accuracy of Pitch Matching Significantly Improved by Live Voice Model," *Journal of Voice* 27 (3): 390.e13–20.

5. Shelagh Davies, 2016, "Training the Transgender Singer: Finding the Voice Inside," https://www.nats.org/_Library/Independent_Voices_Articles/training_transgender_singer-10-2016.pdf.

6. Roni Y. Granot, Rona Israel-Kolatt, Avi Gilboa, and Tsafrir Kolatt, 2013, "Accuracy of Pitch Matching Significantly Improved by Live Voice Model," *Journal of Voice* 27 (3): 390.e13–20.

7. Roni Y. Granot, Rona Israel-Kolatt, Avi Gilboa, and Tsafrir Kolatt, 2013, "Accuracy of Pitch Matching Significantly Improved by Live Voice Model," *Journal of Voice* 27 (3): 390.e13–20.

8. Richard Miller, 1986, *The Structure of Singing* (New York: Schirmer Books).

9. Donald Neuen, 2002, *Choral Concepts: A Text for Conductors* (Boston: Cengage Learning).

10. James Mark Jordan, 2010, *Rehearse!: A Guide and Card Pack to Improve Choral Teaching through Self Evaluation* (Chicago, IL: GIA Publications, Inc.).

11. Harold Swan, 1973, *Choral Conducting: A Symposium* (Upper Saddle River, NJ: Prentice-Hall).

12. Gerald Roderick Knight, 2006, "The Music Philosophies: Choral Concepts, and Rehearsal Practices of Two African American Choral Conductors," in *The Music Philosophies: Choral Concepts, and Rehearsal Practices of Two African American Choral Conductors*. Dissertation, FSU Digital Library.

Five

Musicianship
Developing Notational Literacy

Chapter 5 discusses the importance of musical literacy but focuses specifically on notational reading. Developing the ear and translating that into reading music is addressed. Various methods of teaching notational reading are mentioned as well as sight reading exercises appropriate for novice readers.

"I propose that the reading and understanding of music be taught to our children from the very beginning of their school life; that they learn to participate with enthusiasm in the study of music from kindergarten through high school. No child is tone deaf; every child has the natural ability and desire to assimilate musical ideas and comprehend their combinations into musical forms. Every child can be taught to read music as he or she is taught to read words; and there is no reason why both kinds of reading cannot be taught simultaneously."

—Leonard Bernstein[1]

When we think of literacy, in terms of the ability to read and write, most of us would agree that these skills constitute a critical part of one's education. Being able to read and write are important skills that schools teach to the point of using standardized tests and tying funding and the reputation of the school to the ability to teach these skills. However, the same kind of rigor and standards are rarely applied to music curricula in the United States. With the exception of certain school systems and states, music literacy is not assessed within the profession on a wide-scale basis. Given that music education is an elective subject in many school districts, the urgency for assessment is not a priority for school administrators. Music literacy, insofar as it is limited to note reading and writing, may be absent from many choral rehearsals. Many choirs can and do perform complex music, and many ensemble members do not read music at all. Can you imagine an orchestra or band performing complex classical music while most of their members lack the ability to decode the notes or rhythms? One could argue that some jazz bands have historically performed very complex music without reading standard notation, particularly during its earliest days. Moreover, the harmonies and rhythms of jazz can be very complex compared to some classical genres. Are jazz musicians who do not read standard notation musically illiterate? Are computer applications more literate than some of our most accomplished musicians who are not taught to read standard notation? Having strong musical skills or musical literacy can include the ability to read standard notation. However, if we limit musical literacy to a narrow definition, we may not be able to truly appreciate the richness and diversity of all music.

Have you ever heard the following questions (which really are statements/opinions): Are you a singer or musician? Or have you been in situations where singers were not considered musicians? If you have and disagree with this statement, then the fallacy of this notion, including assumptions that follow this statement, is apparent to you (musicians play instruments and read music and therefore are skilled, whereas singers are not so skilled because anyone can sing complex music). When we think of who is compensated for their services and why, it begins to make more sense. How many paid professional choirs exist in comparison to paid professional orchestras? In the United States, how many choral organizations exist that are on par with any of the full-time major symphony orchestras in terms of compensation and prestige. Why is this disparity the case? When did it start? Why does this disparity still continue? In my opinion, it comes down to how much is invested when music education is introduced into a child's life. As choral musicians and choral educators, we can prioritize what we teach in our classrooms. If we lead a community or church choir, the community must be invested in what we have to offer in a more nuanced way. How many of us have decided to prioritize learning more "songs" at the expense of teaching musical skills not limited to but including music literacy? Unfortunately, I have been guilty of this failure but was lucky enough to have mentors early in my career call my attention to it. Additionally, I began my career in a state that had a sight-reading component as a part of their performance assessment where my failure to teach these skills were exposed to me, my colleagues, and my students. These extrinsic factors helped to reawaken my intrinsic values as an educator. At first it meant that I performed less music and music that was less complex, but in the long run my students benefited from my consistent teaching of music literacy, which I might add goes beyond note reading.

Music literacy insofar as decoding standard notation is important but so is understanding the sociocultural context of the music being performed. In the twenty-first century, it is more important than ever to be able to contextualize the music we select for our choirs. Anyone can google any piece of music we have chosen. If we have done our due diligence in programming, we can bring the world (musically) to our choristers. If we fail to do so, we could find ourselves in a situation where we ignore performance practice or the composer's intentions. A worst-case scenario is when we program objectionable music or find ourselves guilty of cultural appropriation. How many high school choirs still perform Orlando di Lassus' "Matona mia cara" without understanding the translation or context of the piece (it is still on some states' lists)? How many perform music of other cultures without discussing the context of the piece with the choir? How many perform arrangements of "ethnic" pieces by arrangers who have little to no experience with the culture or music that they arrange? Given our technological advances, access to information, and choral scholarship that exist, there really is no excuse for not informing ourselves about the music we program for our ensembles. We are in an age when our ensemble members can research any piece we have selected for them. Often the younger generation is very aware and adept at doing this. Do we want them to be curious about what they are performing? As I stated earlier, musical literacy is very important and more complex than note reading. However, note reading and teaching our choristers how to decode standard notation can be challenging to some choral directors. For the purposes of this chapter, I will focus on the ability to decode standard notation.

In teaching notation, it might be helpful to think about whether we accept Bernstein's assertion that "every child can be taught to read music as he or she is taught to read words; and there is no reason why both kinds of reading cannot be taught simultaneously."[2] If we accept this premise, then we should consider how reading and writing are approached outside of music. Research states that "the development of oral language skills, understanding of the alphabetic principle, and knowledge of print concepts are the greatest predictors of children's future reading ability."[3] The Suzuki method is modeled on similar principles of standard language acquisition (early beginning, listening, repetition, learning with others, encouragement, graded repertoire, and delayed reading). In examining teaching music literacy, specifically the Orff-Shulwerk philosophy, I find learning by rote is valid and reading music notation is an extension of music making.[4] One would think that singing choral music is a natural fit and the easiest venue for teaching note reading. However, many choral singers and directors never get beyond rote learning. Even the Suzuki method is not opposed to learning to read music, albeit delayed. To be clear, labeling and identifying notes do not equate with being able to make sense of notes. A child who can recite their ABCs but cannot read a sentence would not be considered literate, nor should a child who can identify the musical alphabet or label notes be considered musically literate. Labeling should come at the end, not at the beginning; developing aural skills are very important. Indeed, there are a number of ways to accomplish this task.

The Kodály method and Curwen hand signs are effective and have been used for years by many choral directors and music teachers. Scholars such as Dr. Carol Krueger have found other ways to teach notation, specifically to adolescents and adults, which are more updated but still built on the premise that we learn music through hearing and imitating patterns.

Far too often, singers are musically illiterate when they enter the choral setting and directors aren't sure how to develop elementary skills in younger and older singers. Working from the premise that singers learn musical skills in much the same order as they do language skills: we "learn" music through hearing and imitating patterns before reading (translating notation into sound) and writing (translating sound into notation).[5]

In my own practice, I incorporate a variety of techniques to develop musical literacy on the premise that aural and oral skills are fundamental to accomplishing this task. Whatever the system of choice, we should be consistent in its use, whether solfège, numbers, or some other system of developing tonal memory and skills. When developing rhythmic reading skills, Krueger uses the TAKADIMI rhythm pedagogy system, which is an evolution of the use of Gordon's syllables. In my own practice I have found that the Kodály method is easiest for beginners to grasp but would transition to counting as soon as possible. There are a variety of systems to teach music reading, but whatever we choose we must be comfortable with that system and have enough expertise to teach it confidently and be innovative with our approach.

A fundamental concept in music and making sense of music is a steady beat regardless of the system we choose. Establishing that concept usually begins in early childhood, but older singers may need reinforcement in this area. Without a steady beat, teaching rhythm is impossible. Once we are confident that the concept of steady beat is one our singers can grasp, we can explore rhythmic patterns, and it is important to explore them aurally and orally before introducing notation. Rote exercises that introduce rhythmic patterns is one way to prepare our singers for rhythmic reading. When exploring rhythmic patterns and introducing them by rote, it is important to model steady beat and instruct our singers to keep a steady beat. Some may choose to clap rhythms as a way to introduce rhythmic patterns. However, I would encourage engaging the voice as much as possible, which is why I prefer the Kodály or TAKADIMI method to introduce rhythm. Involving the voice in some way can also give our more reluctant singers an opportunity to participate more confidently. In addition to Kodály, you may choose to incorporate Dalcroze as a way to involve the body and further reinforce rhythm and musicality. Whatever system(s) we use to teach rhythm, as well as singing pitch, should be introduced before written notation.

When introducing pitches, we can do so in various ways by rote. With beginners it is important that we give enough without overwhelming them. For example, in solfège practice we may begin with just teaching So-Mi-La, Do-Mi-So, or Do-Re-Mi until they are comfortable with those pitches and their relationship with one another. Then we may incorporate la and fa and finally ti. In my experience I find that Krueger's approach, which is more stepwise than the traditional Kodály approach to teaching solfège, is more practical and fits well with the aurality of our twenty-first-century singers. However, with rote teaching it is easy to incorporate and add pitches rapidly, especially with older singers. Given that the human voice has no exterior mechanical devices to assist with finding pitches, incorporating Curwen hand signs or something kinesthetic will reinforce interval relationship and understanding the contour of scales.

Table 5.1 shows some examples of how we might incorporate aural skills as part of our preparatory exercises in our rehearsals.

Table 5.1   Simon Says Sing

DIRECTOR: Identifies a complex rhythm that will be in one of the scores and performs.	CHOIR: Echoes the director.
DIRECTOR: Identifies complex intervals or melodic passages in the score and performs it on solfège.	CHOIR: Echoes the director.
DIRECTOR: Asks choir to identify either the rhythm or melodic passage within the score.	CHOIR: Searches for the passage and performs these passages while reading notation even though it was previously learned by rote.
DIRECTOR: Rehearses this section and asks choir to identify passages that could be a challenge and asks a volunteer to perform.	CHOIR MEMBER: Demonstrates the passage or rhythm (with help from the director if needed) to the choir and choir performs the passage.

The Simon Says–type exercise in table 5.1, which can fit all age groups, will have to be modified depending on the age, maturity, and experience level of the choir. Other games that can be incorporated are Grace Nash's Echo Chain Game. The Echo Chain Game can be an excellent precursor for incorporating harmony and part independence through teaching solfège. As with the Simon Says exercise, these exercises were designed with children in mind, but we can certainly modify to make them more age-appropriate for older beginners.

When we feel that our singers are ready for note reading, we should simply keep in mind that what they can sing by rote may not be what they can read. When teaching rhythm and reading rhythm, it is crucial to teach what time signatures are. Merely telling our singers that "the quarter note gets the beat" and not explaining why in common time the quarter note gets the beat and that the quarter note outside of that context will lead to problems in understanding other time signatures in the future (think of ensembles that play a piece of music meant to be in cut time in a fast four and how unmusical that is). How many of us have struggled with other meters because we did not learn how time signatures functioned early on? Keep in mind that we would have introduced these patterns in earlier lessons prior to having them perform them.

When teaching pitch, a slow systematic approach should be used. Sometimes it may be worthwhile to have the students speak the solfège while using Curwen hand signs in rhythm prior to singing, given that with solfège they will need to learn this system. Figure 5.1 shares a few simple reading exercises that I would use with beginners. If possible, I would recommend that you project sight reading exercises on a screen or have them use music stands to give your singers free hands for Curwen hand signs and/or keeping a steady beat.

As your singers progress, Sight Reading Factory[6] and similar products may be an efficient way to incorporate sight reading and music reading into your rehearsal. Additionally, if you choose to use solfège as a way to teach pitch, you must decide whether to use fixed or moveable "do" and if you will teach "la"-based minor as opposed to "do"-based minor. The singers will succeed with any system that you are comfortable with. Using numbers

Figure 5.1   Simple sight-reading exercises
https://musicatoakgrove.files.wordpress.com/2013/12/sight-singing1.pdf

to teach pitch is an option and is something that is familiar and easy to understand initially but has its limitations and can become confusing as numbers are used for many things in music including, but not limited to, rhythm and intervals.

Teaching note reading/sight reading in and of itself as a skill has merit; the goal of teaching note reading should be to help our singers become better musicians and apply these skills to the music that they are learning. As our singers develop reading skills, a technique that makes this more practical is to select passages from the music they will be performing. Another technique that can help our singers focus on reading notes (rather than following words) is to teach one or two pieces on solfège. Many of our colleagues teach every piece of music on solfège before teaching text. However, some may find this cumbersome despite its benefits. Teaching one simple piece of music on solfège may be a way to start. If the majority of the

Table 5.2 Rote Meets Note

Introduce short phrases via rote	Use solfège during the preparation/sight reading process to teach pattern.
Introduce the piece	• Explain where "do" is to singers. • If the piece has a motive that is found in each part, have singers identify it in their own part. • Teach everyone the motive on solfège by rote and have singers write in the solfège syllables.
Teaching the parts	• Teach short phrases by rote on solfège and have singers write in the solfège and perform the solfège. • While one part is learning solfège, have the other parts write in the solfège above the notation for their part. • After each section can successfully solfège their part, layer parts. • Choir should be able to solfège the entire piece or section before learning text.

ensemble members lack the skills to do so independently, rote observation may be another avenue. Rote observation can be cumbersome but effective in teaching singers to focus on reading notes rather than following text. Rote observation allows us to teach parts on solfège while students write in the solfège in their parts and learn their music on solfège. This can be an excellent way to reinforce note reading skills. Table 5.2 shows how this would be approached in a middle or high school setting.

Teaching the piece on solfège or a section, even if it is through rote observation, will allow singers to practice solfège and reinforce intervallic relationships. Many older beginners without notational reading skills will be inclined to follow words rather than attempt to decode the notation. This method will allow these novices to follow their part and become familiarized with notation even if they are unable to decode the notation independently. Additionally, whatever system you choose to teach may be reinforced, allowing you to bridge the gap between rote learning and developing the skills to successfully read music independently.

Most of us, including seasoned teachers, understand that we must plan for success. Planning a successful rehearsal is key to student success. We must also be flexible enough to modify the plan based on the ensemble and their reaction to our plan. If we value music reading competency in our singers, then it *must* be included in each of our plans. The following offers four plans (see Appendix 1–4) for various levels based on a method I learned from Dr. Judy Bowers, which was initially focused on choral pacing as a means of classroom management based on the Choksy-Kodály model. Despite its foundation in music education and choral classrooms, I have found this model to be very effective with all the choirs I have worked with.

As choral directors and educators, we have a great deal of influence on what is taught to our ensembles. What they learn, including note reading (more broadly becoming musically literate) is a direct reflection of what our values are. However, in some ensembles note reading is not a priority or even necessary (community choruses and church choirs). We as directors ultimately are left with the decision of what to include in our rehearsals and must be true to our values as well as the mission of our ensembles.

Notes

1. Leonard Bernstein, 2008, *Infinite Variety of Music* (New York: Hal Leonard).
2. Bernstein, *Infinite Variety of Music*.
3. Shannon Kelley, 2021, "Best Practices in Early Childhood Literacy," https://education.uconn.edu/2021/10/20/best-practices-in-early-childhood-literacy/.
4. American Orff-Schulwerk Association, n.d., "Music Literacy," https://aosa.org/about/what-is-orff-schulwerk/music-literacy/.
5. Dr. Carol Kreugar, n.d., "Interest Sessions & Workshops Descriptions," https://www.carolkruegermusic.com/about1.
6. Sight Reading Factory, n.d., "Home Page," https://www.sightreadingfactory.com/.

Six

Program Development
Evolution of the Developing Program

Chapter 6 covers infrastructure considerations and logistics of building a program. Understanding the musical challenges is only part of what is needed. Chapter 6 addresses the logistical challenges of developing school, community, and church choirs (i.e., funding sources, administration, and limitations of each type of ensemble).

"The point is that Art is not an importable commodity. It is not something that can be purchased. If the critics of Art, of musical performance, which is already sort of a contradiction in term, if they become the sort of dictators of what is good or bad rather than the musicians themselves, or rather than the singers themselves, rather than the doers themselves. And if we become a society of critics and consumers rather than of doers, then the Arts are completely betrayed and completely dead."

—Robert Shaw[1]

You have the job and now it's time to get to work! The time to celebrate starting a new position, including the excitement and the enthusiasm that comes, needs to be synthesized into a strategy that builds or develops your program. Developing a strategy to grow and developing a program will never be a one-size-fits-all strategy. For instance, if you are the founding director or inaugural director of a program, the energy, approach, and planning will be different for a program in need of repair or a well-established program. Each one of these scenarios has its opportunities and challenges.

Additionally, the approach will vary depending on the type of choir you are building. A school choir will have very different protocols than a church or community choir. What we can bring to any position are our expertise, vision, and our best effort. This chapter will address various scenarios in school, community, and church choir settings.

School Choirs

> **Scenario 1**
>
> *You have just been hired at a brand new high school that will open in the fall. There is a feeder pattern that you will share with another high school. The expected enrollment of the high school will be approximately two thousand students. The school is located in a socioeconomically diverse suburban neighborhood. The administration appreciates the arts but is focused on science, technology, engineering, mathematics, and athletics. How do you get started?*

Starting at a brand new school or a school that has never had a program can be very exciting and challenging at the same time. One of the biggest benefits is the opportunity to implement your own vision and shape the school culture. However, funding and marketing the program will be a challenge. The principal that opens a new school will also want to make their mark. Moreover, science, technology, engineering, mathematics, and athletics are where the largest investments are made. Despite not having a seat at the head of the table, you are still at the table and can make the program shine. Before you can seriously ask for support, you must be able to demonstrate that you have a successful product. As educators, we understand that music education is not about churning out performers, and performance is only part of what, albeit a very important part of what, we do. However, the administration, faculty, and parents are rarely interested in our philosophy but will certainly appreciate a good performance. In a scenario like this, it is important to have a performance that will leave an impression. Having a good first impression will lead to the right conversations regarding funding, marketing, and securing the support of your administration.

In a new school setting, you may or may not have a modest budget, and purchases would have already been made for the basic needs of the program (risers, piano, sheet music, etc.). However, you may need to secure funding to meet the needs of your program. Funding in most school districts comes from the administration (taxpayer dollars), parent-teacher association, or a booster organization. Each source of funding has its parameters. In my experience, the most restrictive and difficult to secure funding has been funding from the administration, even when they are supportive. Moreover, in a new school it's unlikely that a booster club or a fully functioning parent-teacher association has been established. If you were hired prior to the school opening, then it is possible you were chosen to be the inaugural director: perhaps you may have had the opportunity to advocate for purchases prior to the school's opening. If this is not the case, you will have to make your needs known to the administration as soon as possible. Before requesting funds from the administration, you should have everything prioritized and a justification for the expense. The justification for any expense should be academic, or in some cases a safety concern when approaching the administration. Given the limited funds that most schools have at their disposal, many choral programs rely on booster clubs or similar parent groups to supplement their needs. Booster clubs and similar organizations usually do not have the same restrictions on spending or raising funds that public schools have. However, at a new school a booster club will not exist, and the school parent-teacher association may only be able to offer limited assistance. Establishing a booster club will depend on how successful the program is and whether a vision is marketed to parents who will want to invest in that vision.

Funding is important but a program must be worth funding in the eyes of the students, parents, and administration. At first, we have to market our vision for the program and get buy-in from the students, parents, community, and administration. A new school is one where we have the opportunity to really capture the imagination of the students and build a loyal following. Our musical vision is very important, but we must find ways to uniquely contribute to the identity of the community. When convincing students and their parents to choose between joining chorus or taking another Advanced Placement course, we must ask what our strategy will be. Do we understand the mindset and priorities? Can we make a reasonable case? What can we offer that they can't get from anywhere else? We can offer the students an adult in the building who will get to know them over the course of several years and can advocate for them in a way that most of their science, technology, engineering, and mathematics teachers won't be able to do. Marketing our musical vision is central, but what is most important is that we market ourselves as a resource to the students and community. In many ways, we embody the roles of an athletic coach and academic teacher.

I have found that offering students opportunities they would not otherwise have is an effective marketing strategy. Organizing an annual or biennial tour is an excellent tool for marketing and attracting students. Tours can be performance, adjudicated, or "competitive" tours. Despite my philosophical issues with music viewed as a competitive sport, I have found that competitive tours, particularly those that can garner a lot of press and enthusiasm, have been very effective in marketing my programs. Colleagues of mine have been very successful in capitalizing on being the "champions" at a choir competition. Students, administrators, and parents understand what a first place trophy means. In a new school, bringing home trophies to the administration will definitely secure goodwill and possible financial support. Educationally speaking, adjudication where expert clinicians offer feedback and/or clinics with the ensembles are infinitely more valuable than a contest that offers only a trophy with no feedback. Real growth happens when students receive musical assessment. However, it is possible to make both happen by being judicious about what tour is most appropriate for the ensemble and by building enthusiasm for our program, particularly at a new school.

> **Scenario 2**
>
> *You have been hired as the new director at a Title I middle school of fifteen hundred students. The choral program has been unremarkable at best and generally below average. Enthusiasm for the program is low. Student enrollment in choral classes is very low. You have one choir of forty students, and fifteen of those students were placed in choir or signed up for choir because they need an elective. In addition to choir, you teach two sections of general music and class piano. The administration has hired you to fill the position and appears to have no interest in the program. Maintaining order and raising test scores are the top priorities for the administration. Parent involvement in the school is very low in general, and there is no existing booster club. Can you turn this around?*

In large urban districts, this scenario is often the case. In order to be effective in a position like this, you have to be fully invested in the community, hold your students to high standards, set realistic goals, and truly believe that the arts can make a difference in the lives of students with so many challenges. Personally, it has always been my belief that children who face the most challenging circumstances desperately need the arts for so many reasons. Music may be the place for them to excel, escape, or see a path to a better future. Being in choir may be the first time they achieve at an exceptional level and have a community. In fact, there is evidence that music may be the only thing keeping some students in school despite their academic and socioeconomic challenges.[2] Although this scenario is definitely challenging, it can be the most rewarding experience because over time, we may have the privilege of seeing the lives of these students change before our very eyes. It is one of the places where the impact is seen more dramatically in terms of the social component of choir. However, musically, we must define excellence in accordance with the starting point rather than in comparing ourselves with well-established programs.

In a scenario like this, it is critical that you make alliances with respected teachers within the building, district, and region as soon as possible. If your predecessor has insight that they wish to share, listen with a discerning ear. If you have never taught middle school or "ended up in this job," that is no fault of the students, and you must adjust your mindset. Hopefully, you are there because you love being an educator, working with young people, and you love music; if not, find something else to do. In this kind of scenario, you will likely have very little control over the circumstances you can change within the school year, but you can plan for the next school year while making the best of year one. The first challenge you will have to face is to gain the trust of the students and build morale.

If you have a chorus that has been turned into a "dumping ground," it is frustrating, and you may be thinking "I didn't sign up for this!" Neither did some of the students—but you are the paid professional and they are in your classroom to be educated. Expressing your frustration about the situation, especially with your students when it is unlikely to change, will not help them or you. That approach will only create an antagonistic relationship between you and the students who did not choose to be in choir. Being empathetic and patient with them while having reasonable expectations will at least give you the opportunity to cultivate an unknown love of music. If a student is truly uncooperative, disruptive, and making it impossible for the other students to learn from choir, follow school procedure but be aware of the message you are sending when doing so, if negative behavior is being rewarded by having them removed. In my experience, you can win over many if you have a positive attitude (especially when things are tough) but will alienate the best students with a negative attitude.

Now the stage is set. It is the first day of school and you meet your choir and ask them to sing. Some may burst into laughter, tears, make a mockery of it, there may be silence, or you may get lucky: they will make an honest effort to honor your request. If any of these is the case, don't be discouraged; remember, they are adolescents and have not been part of a singing culture in the past. Their unexpected reactions are less about you and more of a defense mechanism. To mitigate this kind of reaction, before they are asked to sing a single note you have to be real with them. It is important that you empathize with them from the very start: remember singing is a very vulnerable thing to do, especially when you are going through puberty! Preparing students to sing is not about going over the classroom rules and expectations, albeit those are very important; rather, preparing them to sing begins with letting them know that you are not judging them, that whatever sound they make is fine, and that all you are asking them to do is make an effort. Singing complex vocalises or even standard choral vocalises is not a good starting place. You have to remind students that they already love music (perhaps not the music that you were planning to teach), but they undoubtedly listen to music. Talking to them about their musical experiences, without judgment from you or their peers, might be a starting point. When working with middle school students with no choral experience, it might be worthwhile to have them listen and watch choruses their age before asking them to sing together. When they sing together for the first time, it must be as safe as possible. Students must feel emotionally and musically safe, especially at that age and developmental period of their life. The teacher must be responsible for ensuring that the conditions and their classroom is a place where students can be vulnerable.

Depending on the level of buy-in you may have from the students, you may ask them to try to sing a single pitch together. Depending on the size of the group, this can be done with the entire group or smaller groups around the piano. If you are working with exclusively treble voices, G above middle C is a good starting place. If there are cambiatas, for tenors and basses the G below middle C is a good starting place. When working at this basic level, you must model singing and pitch-matching and only use the piano for reference. When demonstrating under these circumstances, it is important to demonstrate with a clear, non-vibrant, well-supported tone. If you are a trained classical singer, this is not the moment to demonstrate your operatic voice. Eventually, you will model more sophisticated singing if you are able to do so, but you are trying to have them match pitch successfully at this point. Once most of them have matched pitch successfully or made an attempt to do so, you may move on to a five-note pattern and/or have them sing a familiar short song together. To accomplish that within the first day or week of school is a success.

Gaining trust and confidence are the building blocks to establishing a culture of singing. As a classroom teacher, you should have a lesson plan and measurable goals (there are sample lesson plans in the appendix of this book to help). If most of the students are trying their best and improving, selecting music appropriate for them is critical. Ensuring that their first public performance is a success will drastically improve their trust in you and will certainly leave an impression on your colleagues and administration even if they were initially apathetic. The greatest reward, in my opinion, is to see the change in students who had no interest in singing begin to enjoy singing and take pride in their choir. That is perhaps the most important accomplishment with middle schoolers in this situation. Once the students begin to be invested in the program, some parents will become involved and by extension the community and administration. However, most of the initial work will be focused on building relationships with your students, parents, and administrators.

> **Scenario 3**
>
> *You have just been hired to lead a successful high school program after the director retires after forty years of teaching. Your predecessor is beloved by the students, administration, and community. The program has strong traditions, a well-established booster club, and has had overnight and sometimes international tours.*

Many educators view this scenario as their dream job, especially if they were a former student of their predecessor. However, if you are an outsider and did not receive the endorsement of your predecessor, this dream could quickly become a nightmare. Many brand new teachers will not have the skills to manage such a large position. Although you may have many of the necessary musical skills from your education, the political astuteness for success may be lacking. The ability to read people as well as having the necessary political skills are just as important as being musically prepared to lead a successful program. Your predecessor in this case may be beloved by most but not everyone. Members of the administration, community, and parents may resent the kind of influence and power they may have wielded. They may view the departure of an influential director as an opportunity to prioritize other areas. An inexperienced, young ambitious teacher could be manipulated if they are too trusting. The ability to decode the true intentions of others, understanding their motivations, and even appearing mature ("old enough") matters. Will it be easy for a parent or senior administrator to celebrate the retirement of a peer (generationally) and in some cases former teacher, only to have someone step into that position who is younger than some of their own children? Will they view this person as a peer or leader in the same way? This is not to say that a young, gifted teacher and musician could not successfully step into this role—many have done so—but it is important to have experienced allies and mentors advise you. They will know the community and the politics more than you will. A younger teacher who has big shoes to fill will benefit from more experienced colleagues. An older inexperienced teacher will only have the benefit of being taken more seriously by some as "more of an adult" with life experience. However, an experienced director (at least five years) who steps into this role will face challenges but will have had the benefit of managing the politics of running a choral program in a less high-stakes environment. They will have likely faced similar "players" before and have made mistakes that they have learned from.

You have just met your enthusiastic choir on the first day of school. The students are anxiously awaiting what you have to say and what your plans are for the school year. Everything seems to be going well; they are excited, cooperative, and ready to make music. You are having a fantastic time, and most of them seem to have accepted you. Eventually you hear the words "Ms. X used to do this" or "Mr. X never asked us to do this." You may feel disappointed or even threatened by hearing this from your students. How do you react? This is a very important question to consider, especially if you are sensitive, insecure, or emotions are running high. Remember that many of your students in this situation will be veteran members and you are the new person. However, you are still the trained professional in the room. When accepting a position with a long and rich history, it is important to do your homework! Knowing your predecessor's history and legacy will make these moments less awkward. Perhaps your predecessor had a great system, and you would like to continue with some aspects of their system. It is important to incorporate your ideas and shape the program in a way that you see fit while respecting the program traditions you have inherited. Over time, you will be able to shape the program without alienating veteran students. After four years, the students will have only known you and the program under your leadership.

An important part of managing an established program is managing the parents. A booster club will likely be very well established and can be a very powerful asset. However, many of the parents will have their own agenda and are only involved because their child is in your program. Your predecessor can be very helpful to you in explaining the dynamics of the booster club you will inherit. Most parents in the booster club are there because they want to help, and many have the skills to do so. It has been my experience that most booster clubs have their own 501(c)(3) status and have more freedom, financially speaking, than your school. Directors usually function in an ex officio capacity. When working with booster clubs, even the most well-meaning and powerful, it is important to remember that their purpose is to boost the choral program. Sometimes young directors may find it intimidating to be assertive with volunteers, but developing a clear vision as well as understanding your role in relation to the booster club will serve you well. Being able to articulate your needs, vision, aspirations, and limitations, and more importantly how it will benefit their children is your most important tool. Finally, keeping a healthy distance from any financial workings of the booster club (avoid handling money if possible!) will minimize misunderstandings regarding your integrity and school policy.

When you inherit a thriving program, the administration is likely to be invested in the success of the program. However, some administrators may be oblivious to the arts and may not prioritize them. In any case, administrators will take interest in the individuals they have hired and their success. Administrators can be great allies but are not friends or peers—they are supervisors no matter how friendly or empathetic they may be. It is critical to develop a cordial relationship with the school administrators in order to be successful. Additionally, relying on more senior faculty members to pitch ideas to or express concerns before approaching the administration would be wise. It is also important to understand the grievance process of your school/district; hopefully, you will never need to think about it during your career but research indicates that issues with the administration and/or parents is one of the leading causes of teacher exodus pre- and postpandemic regardless of the teaching environment (affluent to poor).³ A supportive administration will make our lives much easier but even in a school with a strong program and resources does not guarantee a supportive administration. Conversely, working at a Title I school does not doom one to an unsupportive administration. We cannot control our administration's policies or enthusiasm, but we can be proactive and make decisions about how we will move forward within our school and our careers.

Religious and Community Choirs

Religious and community choirs have similarities and differences. One of the biggest differences is that one is faith-based and the other is based exclusively on musical interest, most of the time. However, some community choirs have a social justice mission or are designed to bring communities together (Gay and Lesbian Association of Choruses/LGBTQIA+ choirs) with music as the common denominator. Many community and religious choirs require or prefer experienced directors with advanced degrees, but not all communities have that luxury. Some will hire less experienced directors, even some without a degree in music, to lead their choirs. Additionally, there are children's religious choirs and professional/community children's choirs outside of the kindergarten to twelfth-grade setting. This section will focus on adult community choirs and religious choirs.

> **Scenario 4**
>
> *You have just been hired to lead a church choir. The church is a community where the average is over sixty-five years of age. There are very few young families, and the pastor has made it a part of her mandate to change this abundantly clear to you in the interview and reminded you of this when you accepted the position. The pastor believes that programming more contemporary rather than more traditional music would assist in this effort and has charged you with this task. However, many of the long-term congregants (who have significantly supported the church financially) and choir members are against this approach and prefer a more traditional choral experience. How do you navigate this dilemma?*

This scenario can be difficult to navigate. If you are working in a church with an autocratic top-down hierarchy in which the church board is mainly an advisory board, then negotiation and working within the framework of the pastor is your only option. If you are in a situation where the church council functions as a board of directors with the pastor as chief executive officer, then the likelihood of finding solutions to address a very valid concern without alienating the congregation and long-term choir members becomes more feasible. In either case, your opinions matter, as well as your artistic expertise, but it will not be the deciding factor on how and if changes will be made. Becoming uncooperative may risk your job. If you fundamentally disagree with the final decision about the role of music in the church where you are employed, then you must plan your exit gracefully. However, if you find yourself in a position where you can be a part of the change, you will have a two-part role garnering support for new musical ideas and explaining to your church leadership what is needed and how realistic it would be to implement changes. In some cases, it is possible to make everyone happy, but in other cases we can only hope for tolerance and patience.

Church politics can be challenging, and as a new music director it is important to understand your function. In this scenario, an overhaul to the music ministry will at best be part of the solution. According to the Pew Research Center, Christian churches have been experiencing a steady decline in attendance, from the silent generation (more religious) to millennials (less religious).[4] Well-meaning church leaders will look for solutions in music ministry despite the fact that music ministry, including programming, will not change this trend. This begs the question: What is the role of music ministry? Is it designed to be entertainment to attract more congregants, or is it meant to enhance worship?

Whatever decisions are made regarding music ministry, its function should always be at the forefront of our planning and thought process. Those of us involved in music ministry, even if we do not share the faith of the congregation we are serving, should have a solid understanding of this function. The role of a music minister is not simply to select music but to be able to explain how it will enhance the congregation's worship experience. Music ministers are not autonomous artistic directors and will often face competing visions especially when newly hired. Navigating these competing forces is possible only if we are flexible, open to new ideas, pragmatic, versatile, and politically astute. There are many congregations that have established cultures, but given the declining numbers of congregants, particularly in Christian churches, you may find yourself in this scenario programming music to please faithful congregants and choir members (an older generation) while trying to attract a younger generation of choir members and congregants.

Community Choirs

Scenario 5
You have just been hired to lead a community choir. They are financially solvent and would like to enrich their programming.

Some of us lead community choirs. For the sake of this chapter, a community choir can be non-auditioned or auditioned, only because the vast majority of the choristers are unpaid volunteers. Leading a community choir and leading a church choir are similar but not the same. When you accept the position, it is important to understand the function of the choir and your role within the community choir. Most community choirs that are financially solvent have a strong board of directors and carefully crafted budgets. Careful stewardship of the budget and strong artistic leadership keeps community choirs alive.

In this situation, you must present an artistic vision that is not only compelling but that demonstrates an understanding and respect for sound financial stewardship. Programming a work that requires massive resources and budget where the onus is on the board to find these resources may not be reasonable. However, if you are willing to compromise or find resources, in the form of favors or bartering of services with other musicians or sharing a concert with another organization, you may be able to realize your artistic vision. Community choirs want to experience high-level artistry, and we as the directors must provide a vision and path to achieving just that. Many board members will support your vision and try to find a way to bring it to fruition. Thinking outside of the box and having a flexible attitude will serve you well in these circumstances.

Auditioned Groups

Whether we audition an ensemble is something we may or may not have a great deal of control over. I think the important question is, Why do we audition individuals for our ensembles? This question is not meant to be rhetorical but philosophical. What is our philosophy behind auditioning? Is it to find a place for everyone in a choir? Is it to keep unskilled singers out of our ensembles? Judy Bowers coined the term "audition in." To "audition in" means finding a place for everyone in our choirs. That does not necessarily mean we cannot or should not have select ensembles. However, it does mean that there are ensembles for everyone. If we choose to audition for placement into ensembles and/or to have an elite ensemble, it is critical to have a fair and transparent process. In the appendix, I will include my audition form as well as other examples.

Auditioning Community and Church Choirs

I grouped community and church choirs together because most of the auditioned choirs are auxiliary groups from within the ensemble and usually do not have separate concerts from the core group. However, in larger organizations there may be independent auditioned choirs from the core group. Moreover, some church and community choirs hold auditions for either admission or placement into the ensemble. I have never led an auditioned community or church group, but I have been a juror for auditioned community groups and select groups within a larger organization.

As a community or church choir director, it is important to determine whether you are going to audition and its purpose. A more exclusive organization designed for skilled singers requires a very different audition from a church or community choir that is open to all. When the organization is more about vocal placement rather than admission, we will be able to find a place for everyone. Auditioning for vocal placement rather than admission does have some challenges. We may need to inform some of our singers that the part they are singing is no longer suitable for them. Some may be resistant to change a part that they have sung for decades. However, by explaining why and presenting it as an opportunity to sing in a more comfortable tessitura and to assist another section rather than making a judgment on their vocal abilities, we may be able to convince the singer that the change is in their best interest. It is important to check in with these singers frequently to make sure they are comfortable with the change as well as surround them with strong singers. The community choir that requires an audition for admission rather than placement has its own challenges.

Moreover, more exclusive organizations generally mandate an audition that we must administer, which is different from the director who instigates an audition where none had previously existed. Community and church choirs with an audition process as part of its admission process have the silent criteria attached to the audition: politics. Given that many if not all members pay dues in the case of community choirs, and choir members belong to the congregation of the church (and likely financially support these organizations), these dynamics come into play. The following offers a few scenarios to consider.

> **Scenario 6**
> *You have accepted a position at an established community choir that has a select ensemble. You must audition each person. Most of the individuals in this select ensemble have been in the ensemble for years and financially support the organization. After hearing the auditions, you feel as though one or several members are no longer a fit based on your artistic vision. You also heard auditions of potential new members who are skilled musicians who can bring fresh energy to the ensemble. How do you handle this situation?*

This situation can be very complex to handle. When there's a board that will give you unconditional support and will respect your artistic choices, coming to a decision will be somewhat easier. But when a board member is one of the individuals that no longer fits your criteria, then you have a challenging task. If board members lobby you to reconsider or invalidate your decisions either directly or indirectly, then you have an even greater challenge. How willing are you to compromise? Is your artistic vision more important than the health of the organization? Will the organization be stronger if you stand firm in your beliefs? Given that each situation is unique and each organization has its own idiosyncrasies, I would not begin to suggest a solution. However, I think it is important to think about the entire picture including the benefits and consequences of whatever decision is made.

Although some church choirs are auditioned, many of those religious choirs are subsets of a larger choir. However, in larger congregations there may be a church choir that is an auditioned group designed to be an outreach choir, or one that is showcased for special services or events. Some of these auditioned choirs may have a mix of paid professionals and skilled singers from the congregation. Depending on the congregation and faith tradition, the auditioned choir could be central to the music ministry or an auxiliary group. If you as director decide to start an auditioned church choir, it would be wise to consult the leadership of your religious organization prior to doing so. However, if this choir has existed prior to your tenure and you are being asked to administer auditions, some political dynamics may come into play.

> **Scenario 7**
> *You have accepted a position at an established church choir that has an auditioned choir made up of professionals and skilled singers in the congregation. After hearing the auditions, you feel as though one or several members are no longer a fit based on your artistic vision. One of the members you are considering rejecting is a relative of the pastor or leader of the congregation. How do you handle this situation?*

In some faith traditions, it is common to have entire families involved in one or many ministries. However, it is important to realize that the pastor of most religious organizations wields considerable amounts of power. If you are new to the position, it will be very difficult to assess how to handle this situation. Moreover, you may feel as though you are empowered to make the musical choices you see fit until a scenario like this presents itself. There are always gray areas, especially when working with church choirs. This scenario can certainly be a vexing situation, forcing us to examine auditioning from a musical and non-musical perspective. A few questions that you should consider for this scenario and for similar situations: Can this individual still contribute to an auditioned ensemble? How can I find a place for them in the ensemble where the other choir members feel as though they deserve to be there, but not as a result of political pressure? Given the individual's position in the church, have the other members already accepted that they have a "reserved" place in the audition ensemble? Are the consequences/benefits worth whatever final decision I arrive to? Will my final decision even matter?

Whether to audition is usually up to each director. Having a sound philosophy, you can readily explain it to stakeholders, which will reduce any controversy regarding the audition results. Whatever your choices, they are your choices, and you are responsible for the choices as the musical leader of the organization. If something does not work or your philosophy changes—that's okay! Most of us have evolved over time. Auditions can give everyone an opportunity to thrive and participate in an ensemble where they can contribute and grow. Ultimately, auditions are not standardized within our profession, and you must believe and defend your system, whatever that may be.

School Choirs

Auditions for school choirs are standard at the secondary level. At the elementary level, auditions also take place, usually for afterschool choirs or professional/community children's choirs. In the appendix, you will find audition forms and audition philosophies for younger choirs. However, this chapter will focus on curricular choirs at the middle and high school levels. Curricular choirs are usually credit-bearing courses, which makes the teacher accountable to the school board and the state as grading affects the grade point average of students as opposed to non-credit-bearing extracurricular choirs. Excluding individuals from curricular ensembles becomes much more problematic, especially if the state or district has a fine arts requirement. However, many of us are able to create space for everyone in a choral ensemble based on skill level. Skill-based auditions allow us to create a space for all our singers. We must be transparent in what skills we assess and be able to explain this to non-musicians such as parents, administrators, and department chairs.

In my experience, I have found that skill-based auditions I believed in and could explain plainly to all stakeholders have minimized tensions when the rosters of ensembles were finalized. Most states have a skill-based audition for admission into an all-state ensemble. I have used the all-state audition process of the states I have lived in to model my audition process, adding my own nuances to that audition process. Basing my audition on the all-state process allowed me more latitude, especially in my early years of teaching, to justify my process and choices. In addition to musically assess their skills, I also had a brief interview for select ensembles. Many choral conductors, including the late Joseph Flummerfelt, believed in evaluating the entire person, including the character of the individual, as part of the audition process for the Westminster Choir.[5]

However, criteria such as personality, fit, and other subjective factors, albeit important factors, for a small intimate select ensemble should not carry as much weight as objective criteria. Moreover, in the twenty-first century one may find it quite difficult to justify decisions in a public school system that weighs heavily on subjective criteria. In some communities, parents are prepared to advocate strongly for their children, and we must be able to explain why one student was chosen for a more advanced ensemble rather than another. Do we really want to explain that this decision was determined by personality or fit? Table 6.1 outlines a few objective and subjective criteria one might consider when determining what we will consider when auditioning our school choirs.

Table 6.1 Audition Criteria

More Objective	More Subjective
Pitch-matching ability	Good ear
Aural memory	Tone color
Intonation	Tone quality
Pitch and rhythmic accuracy	Beauty of timbre
Sight reading ability	Social skills
Attendance record	Motivation
Academic record	Fit for the ensemble

If you choose to use a scoring system, it might be useful to create a rubric for more subjective criteria. When assigning a score to objective criteria, it would be best to find ways to assess these skills empirically, particularly if audition results may create controversy with parents or students. For example, part of the Florida All-State audition requires students to sight read. Students receive a point for each measure that is performed correctly; even when assessing sight reading in this fashion, there can be a gray area. However, if you are ever asked to explain the audition results and you chose to use a scoring system, it will allow you to have empirical evidence to assess a skill. There is no perfect way to audition, but we can try to be consistent and fair with our process.

Notes

1. Robert Shaw, 2024, "His Own Words." Edited by Suzanne Shull, Nola Frink, Douglas Brown, Ellen Dukes, Nick Jones, John Cooledge, Howard Dyck, and Pam Elrod Huffman. RobertShaw.Website. Accessed March 19, 2024. http://robertshaw.website/shaw-quotes.

2. Nicolás Alberto Dosman, 2016, "Why Music Matters in Urban School Districts: The Perspective of Students and Parents of the Celia Cruz High School of Music, Bronx, New York," *Arts Education Policy Review*, 118 (2): 1–16.

3. David T. Marshall, Tim Pressley, Natalie M. Neugebauer, and David M. Shannon, 2022, "Why Teachers Are Leaving and What We Can Do about It," *Phi Delta Kappan*, https://journals.sagepub.com/doi/full/10.1177/00317217221123642.

4. Pew Research Center, 2019, "In U.S., Decline of Christianity Continues at Rapid Pace," https://www.pewresearch.org/religion/2019/10/17/in-u-s-decline-of-christianity-continues-at-rapid-pace/.

5. Alan Zabriskie, 2010, "Evolution of Choral Sound of the St. Olaf Choir and the Westminster Choir," http://purl.flvc.org/fsu/fd/FSU_migr_etd-0673.

Seven

Public Relations
Community versus School Chorus

This chapter discusses the differences in how to garner support for a school chorus versus a community chorus. I will compare the role of a community chorus board of directors with that of a school administration/booster organization in the realm of public relations. I will also examine the impact of the conductor's artistic vision on public relations.

"We are often lured by virtuosity for its own sake, which, though dazzling in appearance, is in fact full of sound and fury and signifies nothing because it springs from no central human or spiritual impulse."

—Joseph Flummerfelt[1]

Whether we direct a school or community chorus, we have the task of growing or at the very least maintaining our program and generating an audience. In an educational setting, chorus is an elective that can satisfy graduation requirements in some cases. Chorus may be a source of community and enjoyment for the students and the community, but its function in a school setting is educational. Conversely, a community choir exists for the sole purpose of the enjoyment of its members and the community. Given the differences between these two circumstances, it is important to speak to each in its own right.

However, both kinds of choruses need to do a degree of marketing and serve their community in some capacity. Although many of us find ourselves in the position of having to do this marketing on our own alone, others may have well-intentioned boards but also difficulty bringing them into focus in a way that truly serves our programs, especially after COVID-19. Despite these challenges, when able we should seek out help in the form of booster clubs, student boards, and boards of directors to ensure that our programs can run efficiently. We cannot and should not do this alone. Chorus America has strategies for reinvigorating (professional/adult) boards as well as strategies for solving common problems that boards face.[2] In a school setting, we generally have to provide more guidance to our booster club and guide our students as they learn to become leaders.

Schools

Schools have a built-in hierarchical structure from the superintendent, school board, principal, faculty, and students as part of the framework. Within that framework, many choruses have a micro-organization within the school. Some choruses have a booster club and student board. Each of these can be very important for recruitment and marketing your program. Booster clubs are a financial resource and are designed to give the choral program financial assistance. Student boards may have access to student club funds that may enhance the extracurricular and social aspects of chorus. Both organizations can express themselves and the needs of the program to an administrator in a way that you as an employee are unable to do. The booster club, in particular, can be very influential with administrators. The power dynamic of a booster president and school principal is very different from an employee/supervisor dynamic. The student board can express their viewpoint but will not have the level of influence that an adult booster president may have. Depending on the administration, they may be entirely dismissive of a student board; therefore, the booster club may be more effective in communicating directly with administration. Despite their limitations, a well-run student board can be a strong asset for you in student recruitment, retention, and communication.

A student board should have a well-defined purpose with specific responsibilities assigned to each board member, which the director monitors. Some student boards are appointed by the director, and the students may go through an interview process. Others are democratically elected by their peers. Some are a compromise between both: students vote but the director has veto power, openly or otherwise. Some may value one way more than another depending on what philosophy they subscribe to. Regardless of the method used to choose a student board, each board member must be responsible and capable of contributing to the board. The director must set criteria for board eligibility to ensure that each board member can contribute to the choral program. Your student board's greatest task is to be the translator and liaison between you and the student body. Whether you are a younger or older teacher, you are an authority figure. Even if you consider yourself hip and are only a few years older than your students, you are not their peer. Student board members can be very helpful in keeping you abreast of the student climate. They can also provide answers to questions you may have regarding their peers' interests and what would be helpful in recruitment. If the student board has access to club funds, they can also enhance the student experience beyond musical experiences. For example, they can use their funds to build community through ice cream socials, pizza parties, and so forth. They may also be able to use their funds to offset extracurricular expenses such as trips, retreats, and so on. See the appendix for examples of how various student boards are structured and organized.

Booster clubs, particularly non-profit organizations, are more complex and the role of director is more of an ex officio capacity than a voting member. Our role is to present our needs to the booster club and to prioritize them. The executive board of a booster club is generally democratically elected by the booster club, but in most cases any parent can be a member. Many booster club parents are professionals in their own right and can mobilize ideas that students (minors) are unable to. The executive board of the booster club wields the most power within the organization and can mobilize the entire booster organization if they have skill set and temperament, and truly support your vision.

Booster clubs often have their own contacts and can use social media to promote your program in ways that may be otherwise limited due to the bureaucratic nature of schools. When booster clubs promote concerts and fundraise via social media, it is wise to check with the administration and school officials to ensure that it is sanctioned by the school. When using the brand of a school for something that is associated with your program, it is crucial that you have oversight. Unnecessary misunderstandings can occur between you and the school administration if social media promotes your event or program in a way not sanctioned by the school, even if it happens without your knowledge. For example, posting images of minors on social media without proper authorization could create issues for you. Proper communication and policies regarding social media and the booster's scope should be established from the onset. As stated earlier, booster clubs' primary purpose is to help you and your organization as long as open communication is maintained. Even though we are ex officio members of the booster clubs, we are still our ensemble and program leaders.

Community Choruses

Community choruses do not have booster clubs, but they generally have a board and an executive committee within that board if they are a 501(c)(3) organization. Community choruses must be self-sustaining, as their mission is primarily musical, and are not part of a larger organization such as a school or church. Unlike a school booster club, we work for the board and the board protects the choir's interests. Many directors of community choruses have been hired by the choir's board. The board is our employer, and our position within that structure is artistic director or a music chief executive officer. We may have a musical vision, but it is subject to a different kind of scrutiny and rigor than most booster clubs would require. A strong board will take necessary steps to ensure the organization's survival. Conversely, a school booster club may advocate for your program to the school board but the powers in a given school system will determine the fate of your program. The booster club can assist with realizing programming that falls outside the scope of the school's means.

Community choir board members are volunteers who donate extra time and extra musical talents to the organization. Most of the board members are professionals in their own rights and will use their skill sets to help the choir run smoothly and stay afloat. As artistic leaders of these organizations, we have to prevent a cogent vision that is also aspirational. We should present our grandest visions while being pragmatic. Many board members join because they want to help bring as much musical magic to the choir as possible. Others are there to help in whatever way they can. Keeping in mind their relation to us, why they are there, and what they need from us, we can successfully manage the administrative side of being a community choir director. We are accountable to them. Most board members want to support our musical visions, and sometimes that means rejecting risky projects or programming that may alienate the choir. Being passionate about a project or programming that the board is skeptical of requires us to convince them that it will benefit the choir. A functional board will ensure that your primary focus is on musical excellence and will manage most logistical and administrative aspects of running a choir. It is truly a luxury to have volunteers with other responsibilities that help you succeed. Because community choirs are not school or religiously affiliated, you have the freedom to program in ways you may not be able to in those settings. Developing interesting and compelling programming is often easier with community choirs because there are very few limits (save the musical ability of the choir) to your vision. The board of a community choir offers you protection in terms of your musical vision because they have vetted your program before the choir has ever sung a note. They represent the choir and will offer you feedback about your programming. They also serve as a source of information when it comes to the history of the organization and will be able to provide data on what programs were successful (in ticket sales, membership, etc.). Although a community choir board is technically our employer, they provide feedback and data other organizations do not provide.

Religious Organizations

Religious organizations rarely have booster groups or a separate board that functions independently as schools do. Some churches may have music committees, but their function is limited to enhancing worship and generally does not focus on music for its own purposes. Some church choirs may have separate concerts and tours, but these are generally within the scope of the mission of the church. Church choir directors are at the mercy of the pastor, church council, and connected choir members. Raising funds for church choirs is often limited to purchasing choir robes and sheet music, or hiring instrumentalists for special services (if the church does not have the budget to do so). Some churches may even be resistant to church choirs raising funds for their own sake as it may take away from other fundraising efforts. Others will be happy to allow the choir to raise funds as this may reduce the strain on the operating budget. Depending on the size, scope, religion, and denomination of the church, having a robust music ministry may or may not be a priority. Some churches will be satisfied with a small choir or cantor accompanied by the organist/music director. Other churches view music as an essential part of the worship experience but have limited funding. If this is the case, the most cost-effective way of raising additional funds is through concerts with a suggested donation or a charge for admission. There is little overhead for these concerts, and almost all of the funds are pure profit. Having a committee of volunteers to help manage a church choir and events like this is more practical than having an organization separate from a booster club. Generally, in church settings many of the choir's needs are funded by the church, but many of our wants are not.

Church choirs (save the Mormon Tabernacle Choir and similar organizations) are not standalone musical organizations. Therefore, recruitment and marketing are focused on your own church community. However, community choirs and school choirs must recruit and market their programs. Many community choirs will want to retain their members and to grow their membership and audience. School choirs must recruit students within their school to join the choir. The survival of the choral program at their schools depends on student enrollment. The community choir and student choir audience attendance often correlate with membership in the ensembles. Most of the attendees at these concerts are connected to each choir member in some way. Granted there are some school or community choirs that have a legacy and can generate an audience because of their popularity, but the majority need their members to market their program. Marketing and advertising only work if you have a product that is worthwhile.

Marketing and advertising must come with the knowledge that you have created art that is worthy of sharing with the public (paying or otherwise). It is essential that we ensure that our ensembles are making the best music they are capable of and that the programming is compelling. In a school setting, it is our responsibility to ensure educationally valuable programming. When giving a preview concert, open dress rehearsal, or work in progress, we should market our concert that specific way. Some audiences will enjoy seeing how music is put together. However, we should not market a concert as ready for prime time if it isn't. Sometimes we may overprogram. If we find ourselves in this situation, it may be better to eliminate a piece (or two) than to make a mess of an entire concert. Our audiences want us to succeed. The best way to market our programs is through successful performances. Success builds on success. People want to support and be a part of successful organizations, musical or otherwise.

Successful concert programming is a major part of the equation in marketing. However, we must dream and dream big, which could involve partnering with another organization to perform a major work. It could be community outreach or a musical tour. It could be all these options and more. We should share our vision and aspirations with our stakeholders. When passionate about our vision, we are likely to convince others to join us in making these dreams happen. Everyone wants to be part of something special that may seem out of the ordinary. Bringing large aspirational projects to fruition and inspiring others will generate enthusiasm within and outside of your organization. Presenting a vision and a means of realizing that vision can mobilize people in ways that we could not imagine. It is better to have lofty goals than none at all. Some goals and dreams can happen in the short term, while others may be long-term goals, but it is important to inspire our choir members and community members.

When we initially accept a position at a school, church, or community choir, most of us are excited to have been hired and have the opportunity to make music and lead a choir. Most of us are not choral directors for the money! However, many of us do not think about what will happen when we leave that position. Sometimes we leave under amicable circumstances; other times we find it necessary to leave or are even forced to leave a position. No matter what the circumstances of our departure, we will undoubtedly leave a mark for better or worse. Even if we leave while dissatisfied with our position, our reputation and legacy follow us. We should think about this matter not when we are ready to leave but when we enthusiastically begin a new position. What is it that we can offer? How can we best serve our community? What could be our greatest contribution to this choir? For each of us, the answers will be different.

Some may say that in a school setting, four-year or otherwise, the students are not ours until all of them under a previous director graduate. This may have a ring of truth to it, but does that mean that we are not going to make our best effort until year four? Does that mean that we give up on those students who studied with our predecessor? Moreover, are we destined to tread water until the "transition period" is over? Or do we try to inspire a love of music and singing in every student that crosses our path? We can and should begin to share all of our musical gifts and talents on day one. We should be our authentic selves and be passionate about what we are doing even if we are not inspiring every member of our choir. Making music for a living is a privilege. When we are excited and passionate about our work, it has the potential to be infectious. Some students may discover their sense of belonging within the school community and society as a result of singing with you in choir. Some may even continue to sing in community or church choirs or become avid concertgoers. To inspire a love for music in young people is in my opinion our greatest legacy.

Community and church choirs generally do not have the turnover rate that school choirs do. Community members and church choir members don't graduate. Some may leave the choir when a new director begins, others may join, but membership in these choirs are quite stable. We must accept that every director before us will have left their imprint on each member of the choir for better or worse. Some of the previous directors may have been beloved and others less so. Whatever the case, we are generally part of the collective identity of the choir and its directors (save being a founding director). Most of us were hired because a group of people saw something special in us and want what they believe we can offer. We leave our legacy to these groups by bringing our unique gifts to the ensemble. We were specifically hired by a church or community choir because they want us to share our talents and believe that under our leadership the choir will thrive. In some cases, we were hired because we were best suited to continue the traditions of the choir. In other cases, we were hired to take the choir in a new direction. Because we are working with adults, most will be cordial even if they are set in their ways. However, some will express their opinions quite openly even if it is at an inopportune moment. Sometimes their feedback will be hard to hear, but remember you were hired for a reason. Over time it is possible to make your mark and realize your vision. Moreover, adults who have the means, experience, and ability may be able to help you in ways you never expected, even if some are resistant at first. If you are genuinely interested in the mission of a community choir or church choir and are a good fit, you will have the ability to not only transform the program but will develop lifelong friendships. Even as we lead a community choir, we are also part of the community. In the case of religious choirs, some of us may direct choirs that differ from our own beliefs, we can still enhance the worship experience for our choir members. Being a choral director in any scenario is to be of service—and to enhance the human experience through music. If we focus on our true mission, then our legacy will write itself.

Note

1. Candice Agree, 2022, "In Their Own Words: Inspiring and Evocative Quotes from Classical Artists Who Died in 2019." *WFMT*, October 22, https://www.wfmt.com/2019/12/30/in-their-own-words-inspiring-and-evocative-quotes-from-classical-artists-who-died-in-2019/.
2. Chorus America, 2023, "How to Get the Best Out of Your Board," https://chorusamerica.org/article/how-get-best-out-your-board.

Eight

Programming Literature
Making Your Choirs Successful

This chapter includes recommended literature for novice choirs and the voicings available, as well as how to incorporate these in a rehearsal plan.

"When we sing something perfectly lovely together . . . and it really clicks, you have this marvelous feeling of brotherhood in the room. We are all human beings. We are all feeling this emotion together at the same time. And this is uniting us. We are not separate."

—Alice Parker[1]

When choosing literature for a choir, you must consider the makeup of your choir. A beginning mixed choir will have very different needs from a beginning treble choir. The maturity level of a beginning adult choir is expected to be different from an elementary choir. Some literature can work for multiple age groups, while many pieces, though simple, may require a degree of maturity. Other pieces of literature may be considered too "young" for adult or mature adolescent groups but could be exciting for children. See table 8.2 for twenty pieces of accessible literature for mixed voices. This list is far from comprehensive, but I have attempted to include a variety of genres, styles, and composers in this very short compilation. Attending conferences and literature sessions are the best means of becoming acquainted with new repertoire. Any pieces listed as SAB should be viewed with caution, which does not necessarily mean that they are suitable for all middle school choruses. When considering the kind of literature I selected for my choir, I always had Bowers' developmental hierarchy in mind (table 8.1).² Even though the focus and audience is middle school, it can be adapted and applied to other choruses.

Table 8.1   Bowers Developmental Hierarchy
1. Sing a melody.
2. Add ostinato.
3. Add a descant.
4. Sing chord roots (Choksy). Add vocal chording when possible.
5. Sing phrases or sections of a round.
6. Sing a round.
7. Sing transition pieces.
8. Sing to two- to four-part songs.

Honoring the composer's intention is a primary consideration, and many of us who have worked with novice choirs, especially changing adolescent voices, have had to ensure that the members of our choirs had options that fit their ever-changing voices. In an educational setting, we must find ways for our students to have a musically meaningful experience while honoring the art that we are teaching them. In my opinion, revoicing and sometimes arranging parts to accommodate the needs of our students and ensemble is perfectly acceptable as long as we do not lose the essential elements or intentions of the composers. If the composer is indeed a living composer, one can certainly email the composer or speak with them about this. In my experience, most are more than understanding when it comes to making their music more accessible for others. Table 8.2 offers an alphabetical order and does not necessarily indicate a particular preference.

"A Distant Shore" is an accessible partner song that can be performed with a mixed choir. If the choir has very little experience with harmony singing, this piece will assist them with developing part-singing skills. In using this piece with a twelve- to fourteen-year-old mixed choir, some notes may be at the extreme range for the changing cisgender male voice. Everyone should learn both songs within "A Distant Shore." If your system is solfège, this piece will allow everyone to learn solfège together. The opening is an original theme, that of "A Distant Shore." The second is the familiar "The Water Is Wide (O Waly, Waly)." Each of these songs is introduced separately and may assist in the development of unison singing skills as well as vowel matching.

Table 8.2 Developmental Choral Music

Piece	Composer/Arranger	Voicing	Age Range	Language
"A Distant Shore"	arr. Mary Donnely and George Strid	Three part with descant	All	English
"Al Shlosha D'Varim"	Allan Naplan	SATB/SA	All	Hebrew
"Al Tambor"	arr. Victor Johnson	SAB	All	Spanish
"Ave Maria"	Franz Schubert/arr. Russ Robinson	SAB	High School/Adult	Latin
"Cantaremos"	Ramon Nobles	SATB	All	Spanish
"Come Live with Pleasure"	G.F. Handel/arr. Patrick Liebergen	SA(t)B	All	English
"Dormi Jesu"	B.E. Boykin	SATB	High School/Adult	Latin
"Durme, Durme"	Audrey Snyder	SATB/3 part mixed	Middle/High School	Ladino
"Festejo de Navidad"	Herbert Bittrich	SATB	High School/Adult	Spanish
"Fōg Elnā Khel"	arr. Salim Bali	SATB	All	Iraqi/Syrian/Arabic
"Gloria"	F.J. Haydn/arr. John Leavitt	SATB	High School/Adult	Latin
"I Dream a World"	André Thomas	SATB	All	English

(continued)

Table 8.2	(continued)			
Piece	Composer/Arranger	Voicing	Age Range	Language
"I Will Rejoice"	G.P. Telemann arr. David and Jean Perry	Three part any combination	All	English or German
"La Voilette"	Susan Brumfield	SSAA	Middle/ High School	French
"Ma Navu"	Audrey Snyder	Three part mixed/ SATB	Middle/ High School	Hebrew
"O Sing With Joyful Pleasure"	J.M. Haydn/arr. Patrick Liebergen	SA(t)B	All	English
"Rhythm of Life"	Cy Coleman arr. Richard Barnes	SATB/SSA	Middle/ High School	English
"Shalom Chaverim"	arr. John Scott	SATB	All	Hebrew
"Shine on Me"	Rollo Dilworth	SATB/SAB	All	English
"Sorida"	Rosephanye Powell	SSAB/ SATB	All	Shona (Zimbabwe)

Note: SAB = Soprano, Alto, Baritone (mixed); SATB = Soprano, Alto, Tenor, Bass (mixed); SSA = Soprano, Soprano, Alto (treble); SSAA = Soprano, Soprano, Alto, Alto (treble); SSAB = Soprano, Soprano, Alto, Baritone (mixed).

    A mixed choir with lower voices may perform either piece without modification, and one theme can feature the upper voice and another section can feature the lower voices. Given that both pieces are relatively short, all singers can experience both themes. "A Distant Shore" reaches its apex when both songs are combined with an optional descant that could be taught to a few singers. It concludes with the introduction of a chord. The elements of line, phrasing, balance, and pure vowels can be taught in this piece. Additionally, "The Water Is Wide" could be used as a solo song for students who may consider future voice lessons or who may decide to sing in a solo festival.

"Al Shlosha D'Varim" is a fail-safe piece. Although it is a Jewish liturgical piece, the translation of this particular version is "The World Is Sustained by Three Things: By truth, by justice, and by peace." Given the translation, it could be considered a non-religious Hebrew text and is accessible for the most novice of choirs. When performing with a mixed choir of very little experience with part singing, I recommend the two-part version be used with the lower voices (alto/bass) singing the A theme and the upper voices (tenor/soprano) singing the B theme.

However, if the choir is a developing choir, comfortable with singing in traditional Soprano, Alto, Tenor, Bass (SATB) harmony, then the SATB version should be used. Although its SATB version is more challenging, it is not too difficult and has many moments for unison singing. The message of "Al Shlosha D'Varim" could fit any season; it is not explicitly a Hanukkah song, nor should it be taught as such. Additionally, the Hebrew should be treated with care and should not be anglicized. One can teach pure vowels without regional accents in the English language. Also, most are long open vowels and the piece can be used to teach long phrases, phrase shape, and choral tone.

"Al Tambor" (based on Al tambor de Alegria or Panameño, Panameño Vida Mia) is an accessible arrangement based on perhaps one of the most popular Panamanian folk songs ever written. It is in the genre of the Panamanian tamborito. Victor Johnson has tastefully set it in three parts. Depending on the range and age of the group, this three-part arrangement may work as written, or one might consider having the basses double the altos while the tenors remain on the bass line. "Al Tambor" can work in many ways and is a three-part mixed range falling within what most middle school mixed choirs can sing. However, voices change and revoicing the piece as mentioned earlier might be appropriate depending on who is in your choir. Although it is set in Spanish, there is not much text to learn. The text and tune are repetitive and easy to learn. The text is non-religious; therefore, it would be most appropriate for school and community choirs.

Regarding the English text underneath the Spanish text: the English text is not a translation of the Spanish text. Given its limited amount of Spanish, I would encourage choirs to perform it in Spanish. In fact, I would go as far as saying that to perform "Al Tambor" in English rather than Spanish is a missed opportunity. Many of us will have native Spanish speakers within our choirs who can assist with pronunciation or in understanding the mechanics of Spanish diction. If your choir does not include Spanish speakers, I am certain there are members of the community who will be able to assist with the Spanish pronunciation, or you can reach out to individuals online for assistance.

"Cantaremos" by Ramón Noble, a Mexican composer, is a very accessible a cappella SATB piece in Spanish. It is non-religious in nature and celebratory, and could be performed by an advanced/intermediate middle school group or a high school/adult choir. The simple tenor and bass lines could fit developing tenor and bass voices. The soprano and alto lines are more challenging. If the treble singers can sing tertial harmonies in tune they should be able to perform this piece.

"Cantaremos," in Spanish, does not contain a significant amount of text. The same suggestion for "Al Tambor" applies to "Cantaremos." Fortunately, it has no English words, which will give us no choice but to sing the piece in the language that it was conceived in. Like any other foreign language piece, learning the translation should be a part of the learning process. Understanding the language would be valuable in communicating the text and musical message of the composer. Throughout the piece, the sopranos and altos move with one another as do the tenors and basses follow suit. There is a homophonic SATB (more legato) section that is not too challenging. The ranges in all parts are limited, and it could be part of the introduction of SATB singing for a novice ensemble.

"Come Live with Pleasure" is an arrangement by the late Patrick Liebergen who was known for arranging music to fit middle school singers in the three-part mixed model. It is labeled as SAB. However, the range and minor adjustments we can make to accommodate our bass clef singers are apparent (octave doubling on certain cadences) without being too disruptive to the voice leading. "Come Live with Pleasure" is non-religious in nature and can be used in school and community settings. Liebergen's arrangement allows younger singers to experience Handel in an accessible musical setting. Given its amount of unison/octave singing and brevity, it allows conductors to focus on diction as well as to explore Baroque performance choices. This arrangement has an optional flute part that could also be played on period instruments such as a recorder. The piano accompaniment could very well be played on harpsichord.

"Come Live with Pleasure" also contains optional solo/small group sections, which can allow for the introduction of simple Baroque ornamentation which one may want to explore with their singers. In my experience, arrangements by Partrick Liebergen are generally accessible for middle school singers, particularly young tenors and basses. The soprano and alto parts also are limited in range as well.

"Durme, Durme" by Audrey Snyder provides younger singers the opportunity to develop legato singing skills as well as to improve their ability to carry longer phrases and shape phrases. "Durme, Durme" may help students learn about the nuances of dissonances and resolving to unison pitches. It would be appropriate for a more sophisticated middle school or developing high school/adult choirs.

The caveat of using "Durme, Durme" in the three-part mixed voicing with older more developed bass clef singers is that the range often is near middle C. Fully developed basses may need other choices. In this case, the SATB version may be more appropriate to use. If there are insufficient bass clef singers to successfully sing the SATB version, it may be wise to revoice, or in cases where the alto has a similar line, to divide the altos.

"Festejo de Navidad" is an Afro-Peruvian-influenced Spanish text set to music by Herbert Bittrich. It is rhythmically challenging but musically accessible for mid-level choirs from high school to adults, especially if the choir is developing their skills in learning harmony. All of its lines are fairly independent, rhythmically speaking. Quasi-polyphonic, it can be useful in developing part independence. Only four measures are homophonic choral writing. Additionally, one can incorporate guitars and percussion for accompaniment, as chord symbols are used rather than the traditional piano accompaniment. There are rhythmic suggestions for both percussion and guitar. If your choir's strengths are language and rhythm, this would be a great fit.

"Fōg Elnā Khel" by Salim Bali is a choral setting of an Iraqi or Syrian tune (depending on the spelling and accent). It is an accessible SATB setting of a Middle Eastern tune. Although it could be sung by a more advanced middle school group, this piece is more appropriate for high school and adult choirs. This is an excellent opportunity to explore non-Western timbres with your ensemble as well as to invite musical experts and community members of a Middle Eastern region to offer their expertise and share their knowledge with the ensemble.

This piece has many unison sections, descant, accessible contrapuntal sections, solo opportunities, as well as homophonic four-part writing with nuanced harmonies. Although not explicitly written, incorporating appropriate Middle Eastern percussion accompaniment with appropriate instruments could bring even more authenticity to this piece. Additionally, listening to the melody in its original form (and to other music in this genre) would benefit the choir.

Vivaldi's "Gloria in Excelsis" from the setting of his "Gloria" is an accessible work for developing choirs. It could be performed by (more advanced) middle school choirs, high school choirs, and adults. In a capable middle school group, one consideration to keep in mind is the vocal range, particularly for the basses. However, one can transpose the lowest notes of the bass line to the upper octave without disrupting the chord structure or voice leading.

Given that "Gloria in Excelsis" is fairly homophonic, it is ideal for teaching on solfège or another system. Additionally, the Latin text allows for teaching pure vowels. When teaching Latin, it is important to be very specific about treating the Latin text and how much anglicization we allow our choruses to sing with.

"I Dream a World" by André Thomas is an accessible piece with text by Langston Hughes. For those looking for a non-religious text with substance, it is ideal. Additionally, it has a clear American identity. It may be performed by middle school through adult choirs; the range is within the limits of the middle school voice, and the primary caveat is to ensure that there are enough tenors and basses to balance the treble voices. It has many unison sections and rich harmonies.

"I Will Rejoice" ("Ich will den Herrn loben") by George Phillipp Telemann, arranged by Dave and Jean Perry, presents an accessible setting for three parts of any combination. The setting is in German with a phonetic pronunciation guide (not an international phonetic alphabet) that English speakers can follow. This guide is helpful, but conductors are encouraged to bring out as much nuance of the German text as possible. The accompaniment is tasteful and stylistic within the bounds of what one would expect for a Baroque setting. Given that "I Will Rejoice" is a canon, balancing all three voices is a higher priority than the traditional expectations of assigning voices.

It is an excellent piece to teach on solfège, engaging everyone all of the time while learning the melody. Although it could be performed by middle school through adult singers, one should be mindful of the range for tenors and basses, which may have limited ranges in both directions. However, this is an excellent choice for a developing choir and allows your ensemble to sing in German without being overwhelmed by the language. Baroque performance practice could also be discussed.

"La Violette" is a setting of an Acadian tune arranged by Susan Brumfield and may seem intimidating given that it is voiced as an Soprano, Soprano, Alto, Alto (SSAA) piece. Some parts double one another, while others are very independent. Additionally, because of its voicing, "La Violette" may also be used with a middle school or high school mixed choir. Middle school cambiata voices can sing the second alto line, while younger baritone or developing tenors can sing the second soprano part alongside treble voices. This setting gives singers more options rather than creating a barrier because of the number of parts. High school or more mature singers may perform this SSAA as written or may decide to perform it as a mixed choir if there are very few tenors and basses in the ensemble.

If all the tenors and basses have changed voices, the director could decide to assign tenors and basses to the second soprano part or have the tenors and basses split and double the first soprano (tenors) and second soprano (basses), respectively. It offers directors choices with limited voices, as well as the French text. The text is not extensive and therefore is an accessible introduction to performing songs in French. Finally, "La Violette" has a percussion accompaniment explicitly notated.

"O Sing with Joyful Pleasure" is based on Johann M. Haydn's "O Herr, ich bin nicht würdig" from Deutsche Messe. Patrick Liebergen's arrangement of Haydn's melody preserves only the primary melody of the piece. The English text, metronome marking, and voicing comprise a total resetting of Haydn. The text has been secularized, which will make the piece less problematic in public school settings. Despite the resetting of this Haydn melody, Liebergen has created a setting (voiced SAB or three-part mixed) that still maintains a classical flavor. Additionally, it could be appropriate for a developing SATB choir. The tenor-bass line includes alternate notes (in octaves) and has a fair degree of independence from the treble line. Treble voices should be able to sing in thirds without much difficulty. This piece would be appropriate for an intermediate middle school, developing high school, or developing adult choir.

"Rhythm of Life" from the Broadway musical *Sweet Charity*, choral setting by Cy Coleman, arranged by Richard Barnes, is accessible for most choirs due to its large unison writing and the way its harmonies are developed. The majority of the harmonies created in this piece are in the form of melody/countermelodies. However, when tertial/tertiary harmony is introduced in the piece, it is presented in a layering fashion where the harmony is layered above the original melody. Given the amount of moving text in this piece, it could be useful in reinforcing skills with diction, particularly with enunciation and the use of clear consonants, outside of the classical canon.

"Rhythm of Life" is accompanied and uses four-hand piano part. However, one can be creative in how to accomplish this as the primo part doubles the choir while the secondo is accompaniment. A mallet percussion instrument could substitute for the piano primo if a second pianist is not available. Although most of the piece is fairly accessible, the last few measures may prove more of a challenge as the parts are denser and require the choir to balance and tune fully fleshed out chords. However, its challenges are not insurmountable for most developing choirs.

"Shalom Chaverim" arranged by John Scott is an accessible work in Hebrew and can be performed by middle school through adult singers. The piece does not have much text and can be an introduction to Hebrew text for an ensemble. When performing the Hebrew text, we should take care to perform it with the correct sounds. In my experience, the word Chaverim must be practiced and enunciated the most as many singers are not accustomed to making the initial [ch] sound.

With the exception of the beginning, most parts are ostinato, canon, and descant. The range may be low for some middle school basses, but one could invert octaves (preferred) and/or transpose the piece to accommodate young basses. Additionally, the descant may be assigned to one or more sopranos with the range to perform this line.

"Shine on Me" by Rollo Dilworth is an accessible gospel piece, which can be performed by middle school singers through adult singers. It allows for the building of part singing. There are unison passages and harmonies are introduced as countermelodies rather than tertial harmony. When the parts are homorhythmic, the top voice is a descant, and the lower voices sing the melody and countermelody. The accompaniment is in the gospel style but not overly complex yet supportive of the vocal line. If one has access to a skilled pianist in improvisation, this accompaniment gives enough information to allow a pianist to embellish.

"Sorida," a Shona song from Zimbabwe set by Rosephanye Powell, has many ostinati and the voicing that could work for most choirs ranging from middle school to adults. The Soprano, Soprano, Alto, Baritone (SSAB)version is best taught when there are limited numbers of lower voices to balance the treble voices. In addition to ostinati used to create harmony, tertial harmony is introduced by layers, and the top vocal line is an upper harmony rather than melodic. Powell includes detailed performance notes as well as appropriate percussion accompaniment and percussion instruments.

Notes

1. Frank J. Oteri, 2022, "Alice Parker: Feeling the Same Emotion at the Same Time—New Music USA." *New Music USA*, February 28, https://newmusicusa.org/nmbx/alice-parker-feeling-the-same-emotion-at-the-same-time/.

2. Frank Abrahams, Judy K. Bowers, Paul Head, James Jordan, Patrick Liebergen, and Sherri Porterfield, 2011, *Teaching Music through Performance in Middle School Choir* (Chicago: Gia Publications, Inc.).

Appendix
A Note about COVID-19

Choral Music in a Post-COVID-19 World

In 2020, COVID-19 changed the world and profession for the foreseeable future. In a post-COVID-19 world, many directors may have to build or rebuild their programs. In some cases, choral programs may have to start from zero. Generating interest, commitment, and enthusiasm will not be fully realized until members feel as though singing in a choral ensemble is safe and enjoyable.

At the beginning of the pandemic, the American Choral Directors Association and National Association of Teachers of Singing presented a webinar, "A Conversation: What Do Science and Data Say about the Near Term Future of Singing," in May of 2020 to address the future of singing during the pandemic. To some, the webinar was devastating to choral music and singing in general. In March 2020, a choir in Mount Vernon, Washington, had an outbreak in which forty-five of its members were infected: three were hospitalized and two passed away. Stories like these were at the top of national headlines and perhaps cemented an already bleak outlook for the future of choral music. As the world shut down, it was clear that choral music would suffer considerably and may be one of the last things to return to society. Some choral groups embraced the virtual choir format, while others suspended activities indefinitely. Choirs that chose to continue to meet in person for the most part sang with masks on and often in outdoor venues. A few choirs performed indoors, many without a live audience. Streaming concerts, virtual choirs, and outdoor concerts became the norm in a COVID-19 world for much of the choral profession.

Given the role that technology has played in the pandemic, Generations Z and Alpha are certainly more technologically adept than previous generations and are likely to be better equipped to face the challenges that the COVID-19 pandemic presented to the choral community. Moving to online choral/musical instruction and music making through technology is not what anyone had necessarily expected, but it was the only way that music making was able to continue. As vaccines became more widely available and distributed, COVID-19 rates declined. However, COVID-19 outbreaks can and will continue to occur in the foreseeable future, and although disruptive, it is more manageable and less deadly.

As of 2022, the world has learned to manage rather than eradicate COVID-19. Depending on the situation, some organizations have returned to singing and music making with no restrictions, in what appears to be normal circumstances (pre-COVID-19). Other organizations require masks and/or vaccinations, boosters, or some combination of both. Some monitor community transmission rates to determine policy while others must follow US Centers for Disease Control and Prevention or negotiated union protocols, whether they are teachers' unions or musicians' unions. The post-COVID-19 world has presented new challenges that could not be predicted, and there are no clear national or consistent local policies.

Despite the progress that has been made in managing COVID-19, choral directors are still rebuilding or building their choral ensembles. As we have returned to in-person learning, many educators are managing musical and social learning gaps. Many recent college graduates will have missed the opportunity of student teaching experiences in a choral setting, singing in ensembles, or rehearsing ensembles in what is typically the final year of their studies. Furthermore, many may not have had the benefit of mentorship usually provided by their cooperating instructors before they are tasked with leading their own ensembles.

Many choral directors will likely bring the skills they have acquired as a result of the pandemic and integrate it into their programs. Experienced directors who have had years of practice and building programs will find a way to make this happen seamlessly. However, recent graduates will not have had the kinds of experiences that prior generations had in their preparation. Many recent graduates majoring in music education will likely lead a choral program in a school setting without the guidance or insight of traditional practicum experiences and mentorship that comes with it. Graduates near the end of their studies during the height of COVID-19 would likely have graduated without full-time internship, which is usually the capstone experience of most undergraduate music education programs. Conferences, professional development, and bonding with their cohorts, as well as traditional in-person networking, have been altered because of COVID-19.

Post-COVID-19 graduates will have to integrate technological skills with their musical training in a way that has never been done before. Choral directors entering the profession of education will undoubtedly encounter a profession different from the one they were prepared for. However, those who graduate further out from the onset of the pandemic may have a more "normal" educational experience. Despite returning to a normality, COVID-19 and its disruption will likely affect the profession for years to come.

Appendix 1
School Choir Lesson Plan

Based on Kodály-Choksy Model[1]
Fifty-minute plan

Objective: Students will be able to _____

National/State/District Standards Addressed: _____

Materials: _____

Pre-Activity (Do Now):
(Try to reinforce previously learned material in Do Now)

1. Vocal exercise (fifteen minutes maximum)—inner hearing, solfège drill, sight reading, vocal technique:
   Vocal exercise #1:   purpose:
   Vocal exercise #2:   purpose:
   Vocal exercise #3:   purpose:
   Vocal exercise #4:   purpose:

2. Most difficult piece or task: ten minutes (usually new difficult information).
   Task: _____

3. Review/Polish previous materials: ten minutes (reinforce previous skills).
   Task: _____

Announcement/nonmusical issues

4. Introduce new easy material: Five to ten minutes (easy to grasp).
   Task: _____

5. Favorite piece or activity: Five to ten minutes. Have fun! (their comfort zone).

6. Summarize: two minutes. We accomplished/homework is?

7. Offer individual assistance: five minutes.

Assessment: Students were able to _____
Students need reinforcement in _____

Homework: At home students should _____

Note

1. Judy Bowers conference presentation. Judy Bowers, 2017, "Maine American Choral Directors Association Presentation, 2017" (Gorham, ME).

Appendix 2
School Choir Lesson Plan

Based on Kodály-Chosky Model[1]
Ninety-minute plan

Objective: Students will be able to _____

National/State/District Standards Addressed: _____
Materials: _____

Pre-Activity (Do Now):
(Try to reinforce previously learned material in Do Now)

1. Vocalizations (fifteen minutes maximum)—vocal technique:
   Vocal exercise #1:   purpose:
   Vocal exercise #2:   purpose:
   Vocal exercise #3:   purpose:
   Vocal exercise #4:   purpose:

2. Musicianship (ten minutes): inner hearing, solfège drill, sight reading.
   Preparatory exercise (ear training, dictation, and/or echo chain game like exercises):
   Rhythmic reading
   Sight-singing

3. Most difficult piece or task: twenty minutes (usually new difficult information).
   Task: _____
   Announcement/nonmusical issues

4. Review/Polish previous materials: fifteen minutes (reinforce previous skills).
   Task: _____

5. Introduce new easy materials: five to ten minutes (easy to grasp).
   Task: _____

6. Favorite piece or activity: five to ten minutes. Have fun! (their comfort zone).

7. Summarize: five minutes. We accomplished/homework is?

8. Offer individual assistance: five minutes.

Assessment: Students were able to _____
Students need reinforcement in _____

Homework: At home students should _____

Note

1. Judy Bowers presentation. Judy Bowers, 2017, "Maine American Choral Directors Association Presentation, 2017," (Gorham, ME).

Appendix 3
Church Choir Plan

Two-hour rehearsal

Objective: _____

Pieces: _____

Pre-Rehearsal: Prayer led by choir member

1. Vocal exercise (fifteen minutes maximum)—vocal technique and musical development:
   Vocal exercise #1:   purpose:
   Vocal exercise #2:   purpose:
   Musical prep. #3:   purpose:
   Musical prep. #4:   purpose:

2. Most difficult piece or priority anthem: thirty minutes (usually new difficult information).
   Task: _____

3. Review/polish previous materials: twenty-five minutes (reinforce previous skills).
   Task: _____
   Announcement/non-musical issues/break Ten minutes.

4. Introduce new easy material: twenty minutes (easy to grasp).
   Task: _____

5. Favorite piece or activity: twenty minutes. Their comfort zone/they enjoy the most.

Appendix 4
Community Choir Plan

Two-hour rehearsal

Objective: _____

Pieces: _____

1. Vocal exercise (fifteen minutes maximum)—vocal technique and musical development:

   Vocal exercise #1:   purpose:
   Vocal exercise #2:   purpose:
   Musical prep. #3:   purpose:
   Musical prep. #4:   purpose:

2. Most difficult piece or task: thirty minutes (usually new difficult information).
   Task: _____

3. Review/polish previous materials: twenty-five minutes (reinforce previous skills.)
   Task: _____

Announcement/nonmusical issues/break Ten minutes

4. Introduce new easy material: twenty minutes (easy to grasp).
   Task: _____

5. 5. Favorite piece or activity: twenty minutes. Their comfort zone/they enjoy the most.

Appendix 5
Audition Form A—High School/Middle School (Dosman)

Vocal-Musical Quality *Thirty points*
Tone quality ____ out of 10
Intonation _____ out of 10
Musicality of prepared piece ____ out of 10
Comments:
Musical Skills *Sixty-two points*
Sight Reading (thirty-two points)
Example 1 ____ out of eight measures performed correctly
Example 2 ____ out of eight
Example 3 ____ out of eight
Example 4 ____ out of eight
Aural Matching (thirty points)
Example 1 ____ out of ten (ten accurate/zero inaccurate)
Example 2 ____ out of ten
Example 3 ____ out of ten
Interview *Eight points*
Comments:

Audition Form A—High School/Middle School (Dosman)

The vocal musical quality and interview score are the most subjective components of this form. Intonation is perhaps the most objective in these categories. Regarding the interview, character, enthusiasm, and interest in the ensemble are evaluated. This receives the lowest score as it is the most subjective part of the audition. The musical skills that are evaluated are the most objective. Each sight reading example is eight measures and becomes progressively more difficult (based on Florida All-State sight reading). Post-COVID-19, I have had students submit their prepared solo in advance via video to give them the best opportunity to showcase their vocal ability.

Appendix 6
Audition Form B—High School[1]

This audition form is used by the Minnesota Music Educators Association for their all-state auditions. Vocal quality is the primary value, which is apparent in the scoring system. However, note accuracy, rhythmic accuracy, and diction are also scored. Additionally, scales are a part of their criteria. This is not an empirical system but clearly demonstrates what is valued in the audition. If you choose to use a form like this, a qualitative narrative is appropriate for explaining the scores to students, parents, and administrators.

Note

1. Minnesota Music Educators Association, 2022, "Vocal Rubric," https://mmea.org/wp-content/uploads/2022/08/Vocal-Rubric-2022.docx-1-1.pdf.

MMEA ALL-STATE VOCAL AUDITIONS (revised September 2022)   Audition ID: _____

PART ONE: SOLO

Criteria	Score	Maximum
Tone Quality:	_____	/ 15
Vocal Technique:	_____	/ 10
Rhythmic Technique:	_____	/ 10
Diction:	_____	/ 10
Intonation:	_____	/ 10
Musicianship:	_____	/ 10
Total:		/ 65

Comments for solo:

PART TWO: Alma del Coré

Criteria	Score	Maximum
Rhythmic Accuracy:		/ 10
Note Accuracy & Intonation:		/ 10
Diction:		/ 5
Total:		/ 25

Comments for required art song:

PART THREE: SCALES

	Score	Maximum
Ascending:	_____	/ 5
Descending:	_____	/ 5
Total:		/ 10

Comments for scales:

Judge's Comments:

Total Score: _____

(100 points possible)

Judge's signature:

Appendix 7
Audition Form A—Elementary[1]

Note: Bartle does not quantify the audition criteria. However, Bartle does specify priorities in the audition process. One can quantify this form if they desire, but I have interpreted these criteria to be more qualitative in nature. Given the time the book was published as well as the background of the composer, I would avoid including number six as the language used could be interpreted as non-inclusive—the language could also call Americans with Disabilities Act compliance into question. Additionally, number four could be viewed as somewhat problematic, but it does assess an academic skill. The following are Jean Ashworth Bartle's audition priorities for auditioning children. These are listed in order of importance:

- High degree of motivation
- A good musical ear
- A pleasant voice
- An ability to read a language
- Self-reliance
- Good physical health
- Self-reliance
- Social skills

The language of this is subjective and would require a qualitative description of each category. Given the limited skills and knowledge that children have acquired, a descriptive nature would be more appropriate as well as including criteria that evaluate social and academic skills.

Note

1. Based on Jean Ashworth Bartle, 1993, *Lifeline for Children's Choir Directors* (New York: Alfred Music).

Appendix 8
Audition Form B—Elementary[1]

Part 1: Vocal Exercises					
	Four Points	*Three Points*	*Two Points*	*One Point*	*Zero Points*
Tone Quality	Utilizes clear, centered, rich head voice for entire exercise. No pushing/ sliding.	Head voice is used for entire exercise, but tone is breathy or thin. No pushing/ sliding.	Head voice is present, but chest voice is used at inappropriate places. Tone is raspy and/or unsupported.	Chest voice/ pop style is used more frequently than head voice. Tone is pushed or strained.	Exercise cannot be completed accurately due to use of speaking voice, pitch-matching issues. Exercise is not completed at all.
Vowel Placement and Formation	Consistently utilizes tall, rounded, forward-placed vowels.	Consistently utilizes tall vowels; placement is occasionally nasal or pulled back, but not consistently.	Tall vowels are utilized some of the time, but not consistently. Placement is consistently pulled back or nasal.	Vowels are consistently spread or closed. Placement is almost always pulled back or nasal.	Does not complete exercise.

(continued)

Part 2: Tonal Melodies					
	Four Points	Three Points	Two Points	One Point	Zero Points
Intonation/ Pitch Accuracy			Pitches are sung correctly and in tune for the entire exercise.	One or two pitch errors or pitches are sung correctly, but there are occasional intonation issues.	Three or more errors in pitch accuracy. Pitches are frequently out of tune.
Part 3: Partner Song					
Independence			Correctly sings assigned melody with no pitch or rhythmic alterations.	Maintains assigned melody with one or two notable errors in pitch or rhythmic accuracy.	Performs assigned melody with three or more notable errors in pitch or rhythmic accuracy. Utilizes speaking voice at any time. Melody is difficult to discern.
Part 4: Dona Nobis Pacem					
Style			Consistently demonstrates tone quality, placement, and vowel shapes consistent with bel canto style singing.	Demonstrates understanding of tone quality, placement, and vowel shapes consistent with bel canto style singing, but does not apply it consistently.	Does not demonstrate tone quality, placement, and vowel shapes consistent with bel canto style singing.

	Four Points	Three Points	Two Points	One Point	Zero Points
Breath Control/ Phrasing			Holds notes to full rhythmic value and maintains four-bar phrases with no errors.	Generally holds notes to full rhythmic value and maintains four-bar phrases, but with one or two notable errors.	Demonstrates three or more errors in rhythmic value/ phrasing. Does not consistently hold notes to full value or maintain four-bar phrases.
Intonation/ Pitch Accuracy			Accurate pitch and intonation for entire exercise.	Two or three pitch or intonation errors.	Four or more errors in pitch accuracy.
Rhythmic Accuracy			Accurate rhythm throughout; maintains prescribed steady tempo throughout.	One to three rhythm errors. Maintains steady tempo at faster or slower than eighty-six to ninety-two beats per minute.	Four or more rhythm errors. Does not maintain steady tempo.

The Florida Music Educators Association is one of the states that provides an auditioned all-state experience for elementary-aged children (grades four to six). This rubric defines the scoring system clearly and has multiple components of evaluation. This form is more objective in nature and places a high value on tone quality and vowel placement, which is more subjective. However, it clearly defines what is considered appropriate tone for the ensemble. Although pitch rhythm and breath control are not empirically measured with specificity, this rubric gives a range as to where the scores will fall within the rubric. This system can be modified and adjusted for other ensembles and adjusted to reflect one's values as far as tone and vowel placement.

Note

1. Florida Music Educator Association, n.d., "All-State Audition Rubric," https://img1.wsimg.com/blobby/go/f8b4018b-c20b-4bf6-aa8d-32bcf3b14aea/downloads/FMEA%20All%20State%20Elementary%20Chorus%20Audition%20Rubr.pdf?ver=1699832366122.

Selected Bibliography

Abrahams, Frank, Judy K. Bowers, Paul Head, James Jordan, Patrick Liebergen, and Sherri Porterfield. 2011. *Teaching Music through Performance in Middle School Choir*. New York: GIA Publications.

American Orff-Schulwerk Association. n.d. "Music Literacy." https://aosa.org/about/what-is-orff-schulwerk/music-literacy/.

Carol K. Krueger Music. n.d. "Session and Workshops." https://www.carolkruegermusic.com/about1.

Chorus America. 2023. "How to Get the Best Out of Your Board | ChorusAmerica." https://chorusamerica.org/article/how-get-best-out-your-board.

Davies, Shelagh, Viktória G. Papp, and Christella Antoni. 2015. "Voice and Communication Change for Gender Nonconforming Individuals: Giving Voice to the Person Inside." *International Journal of Transgenderism* 16 (3): 117–59.

Decker, Harold A., and Julius Herford. 1973. *Choral Conducting: A Symposium*. Upper Saddle River, NJ: Prentice Hall.

Dosman, Nicolás Alberto. 2017. "Why Music Matters in Urban School Districts: The Perspectives of Students and Parents of the Celia Cruz High School of Music, Bronx, New York." *Arts Education Policy Review* 118 (2): 67–82.

Garrett, Marques L. A. (Ed.). 2023. *Oxford Book of Choral Music by Black Composers*. Oxford: Oxford University Press.

Granot, Roni Y., Rona Israel-Kolatt, Avi Gilboa, and Tsafrir Kolatt. 2013. "Accuracy of Pitch Matching Significantly Improved by Live Voice Model." *Journal of Voice* 27 (3): 390.e13–20.

Jennings, Kenneth. 1982. *Sing Legato*. San Diego: Neil A Kjos Music Company.

Jones, Stefanie Dion. 2021. "Best Practices in Early Childhood Literacy." https://education.uconn.edu/2021/10/20/best-practices-in-early-childhood-literacy/.

Jordan, James. 2010. *Evoking Sound Rehearse! A Guide and Card Pack to Improve Choral Teaching through Self-Evaluation*. New York: GIA Publications.

Knight, Gerald R. 2006. "The Music Philosophies, Choral Concepts, and Rehearsal Practices of Two African American Choral Conductors." https://diginole.lib.fsu.edu/islandora/object/fsu:181107/datastream/PDF/view.

Marshall, David T., Tim Pressley, Natalie M. Neugebauer, and David M. Shannon. 2022. "Why Teachers Are Leaving and What We Can Do about It." *Phi Delta Kappan* 104 (1): 6–11.

Miller, Richard. 1996. *The Structure of Singing: System and Art in Vocal Technique*. Boston: Schirmer Cengage Learning.

Nash, Grace. *Echo Chain Singing Games*. Swartwout Prod., Sedona, AZ.

Neuen, Donald. 2002. *Choral Concepts*. New York: Schirmer Books.

Palkki, Joshua. 2017. "Inclusivity in Action: Transgender Students in the Choral Classroom." *Choral Journal* (57) 11: 10–34.

Sight Reading Factory. 2018. "Practice Sight Reading and Sight Singing Exercises Online—Sight Reading Factory." https://www.sightreadingfactory.com/.

Swan, Harold. 1973. *Choral Conducting: A Symposium*. Hoboken, NJ: Prentice-Hall, Inc.

Thomas, André J. 2007. *Way Over in Beulah Lan': Understanding and Performing the Negro Spiritual*. Dayton, OH: Heritage Music Press.

The Trevor Project. 2020. "The Trevor Project—Saving Young LGBTQ Lives." https://www.thetrevorproject.org/.

Zabriskie, Alan. 2010. "Evolution of Choral Sound of the St. Olaf Choir and the Westminster Choir." http://purl.flvc.org/fsu/fd/FSU_migr_etd-0673.

Index

Page references for figures and tables are italicized.

ACDA. *See* American Choral Directors Association
adolescent choirs. *See* high school choirs; middle school choirs
African American choral tradition, 15–17; African American choral repertoire, *111–12*
American Choral Directors Association (ACDA), 13, 16, 121
appoggio. *See* breath management
attire, 20, 22
auditions, 92–97; criteria, *97*; forms, 135, *136*, 137–38, *139–41*, 141–42

BIPOC. *See* diversity
blend, 41, 55, 59, *60–61*, 61, 74–75; historic choral schools, *60–61*; sonic unity, 56
board of directors, 90–91, 99–102
booster clubs, 81, *83*, *86*, 88, 100–104
Bowers, Judy, 78, 92, *110*
breath management, 39–40, 49, 51–53; exercises, *54*

children choirs. *See* elementary choirs
choir parents, 28–32, 45, 80, 82, 86, 96–97
Choksy, 78, *110*
Chorus America, 100
church choirs, 27–28, 33–35, 58–59, 70, 79–80, *89*, 90–95
church pastors, interacting with, 33, *89*, 90, 94, 104
classroom management, 30, 51, 78
community choirs, 27–28, 35–37, 58–59, 70
concerts, 5, 14, 29, 34–36, 101, 104–5, 121
conducting, 2–11, 16, 59
conducting degrees. *See* professional preparation
conferences. *See* professional preparation
count-singing, 65–66
COVID-19, 57, 100, 121–23, 134
Curwen hand signs, 62, 72, 74–75

developing choirs, 32, 34, 39, 42, 52, 61, 64, 67, 79, *110*, 113–18
diction, *60–61*, 65, 114–15, 118
diversity, 12, 13–23, 70

ear training, 29, 63, 127
elementary choirs, 28–31, 40–41, 72, 109, 137–42

faith-based choirs. *See* church choirs
falsetto, 21, 42, 46–47
females, 20, 41–42, 46–47, 66
Flummerfelt, Joseph, 96, 99

harmony, 75, 110, 113, 115, 118–19
high school choirs, 28–32, 35, 44–45, 62, 69, 71, 77, *80*, *86*, 95, *111–12*, 114–18, *133*, 134, 135, *136*
human connection, 1–3, 5, 7, 9

IPA. *See* International Phonetic Alphabet
International Phonetic Alphabet (IPA), 58, 117
intonation, 39, 64, 67, *97*, *133*, 134, *140–41*

kinesthetic, 42, 46, 74
Kodály, 62, 72–73, 78
Krueger, Carol, 72–73

Lesbian, Gay, Bisexual, Transgender, Questioning (LGBTQ), 13, 19–24, 35, 89
lesson planning, 85, 125–28

males, 14–15, 31, 41–42, 46–47
middle school choirs, 22, 29–31, 41, 44–45, 62, 83, 85–86, 109–20, *133*, 134
mixed choir, 109–17
monotone, 41–42
musical literacy. *See* notational literacy
musicianship, 5, 29, 65, 69, 71, 73, 75, 135

National Association for Music Education (NAfME), 16
National Collegiate Choral Organization (NCCO), 13–14
notational literacy, 61–62, 65, 67, 69, 71, 73, 75, 77; sight-singing exercises, *76*

Orff, 72

pacing, 29–30, 78
Palkki, Joshua, 19–20, 30–31
philosophy, 2, 16, 23, 29, 40, *60–61*, 72, 92, 101
pitch-matching, 39–49, 85, *97*, *139*
politics, 87, 90, 93
posture, 40, 49–54; choral singing postures, *50*
professional preparation, 5–6, 13–15, 89, 109
programming, 14–18, 23, 32–36, 49, 71, *89*, 90–91, *91*, 103, 105, 109
public relations, 99, 101, 103, 105, 107

rehearsal priorities, 39, 64
repertoire, 14, 18, 30, 32, 34–35, 72, 109
rhythm, 34, *60–61*, 64–66, 70, 73, *74*, 75, *97*
rote, 72–77; rote to notation, *77*

selecting music. *See* repertoire
Shaw, Robert, 2, 59, *61*, 65, 79
sight-singing. *See* notational literacy
skill development, 39–67, 72, *110*, *111–12*
social justice, 13, 35, 89

solfège, 62, 73–77, 110, 116–17, 127
soprano, alto, baritone (SAB). *See* mixed chorus
soprano, alto, tenor, bass (SATB). *See* mixed chorus
soprano, soprano, alto, alto (SSA/A). *See* treble voices
struggling singers, 43–49
student boards, 100–101
Suzuki, 72

Thomas, André, 1, 17, 59, 64, *111*, 118
tone, 39–45, 48–51, 55, 58–59, *60–61*, 65, 67, 69, 85, *97*, 113, *133, 139–41*, 142
tone-deaf, 41–42
tours, 82, *86*, 103–4

transgendered singers, 19–23, 41–43, 48
treble voices, 20, 58, 67, 85, 117–19

uniforms. *See* attire
unison singing, 39, *60*, 113–19

vibrato, *60*, 67
vocalizations, 40, 55, 57–59, *60*, 127
vocal technique, 40, 58–59, 64
voice changes, 41, 45, 47
vowels, 56, 57–58, *60*, 64–65, 112–13, 116

warm-ups. *See* vocalizations
Westminster Choir, *60*, 96
worship, 90–91, 103–4, 107

About the Author

Dr. **Nicolás Alberto Dosman** is director of choirs and assistant professor of teaching at the University of California, Davis. Prior to his appointment at University of California, Davis, he was associate professor of music-choral conducting and director of choral studies at the University of Southern Maine, Osher School of Music. Under his leadership, the University of Southern Maine Chamber Singers performed at the 2022 American Choral Directors Association Eastern Region Conference and the Osher Choral Union as the University of Southern Maine made its Carnegie Hall debut.

In addition to his academic responsibilities, Dosman was chorus master for the Portland Symphony Orchestra's Magic of Christmas series and served as chorus master for Opera Maine. On the international stage, Dosman was a headliner at the Encuentro Latinoamericano de Música Coral in the Republic of Panama and the Canta Cantemus Festival Chorus in Mexico, and was a presenter in Athens, Greece. He is scheduled to conduct in Vienna and Salzburg in 2024.

Prior to his tenure at the University of Southern Maine, he was the director of choral activities and applied voice at Colby College. He was a conducting fellow with the Continuo Arts Foundation (Westfield, New Jersey) and was also the director of Casita Sings Children's Chorus (Bronx, New York). He founded the Miami Choral Festival in 2008 and was also the chairman of the Miami-Dade/Monroe County region of the Florida Vocal Association while serving as a public school teacher. He holds degrees from Teachers College, Columbia University, Florida State University, and the Oberlin College Conservatory of Music.

www.ingramcontent.com/pod-product-compliance
Lightning Source LLC
Chambersburg PA
CBHW020741230426
43665CB00009B/520